THE GRAND REBEL

THE GRAND REBEL

An Impression of Shivaji
Founder of the Maratha Empire

BY

DENNIS KINCAID

GYAN

Published by

GYAN

Gyan Publishing House
5, Ansari Road
Daryaganj, New Delhi-110002
Phone: 011-47034999, 9811692060
E-mail: books@gyanbooks.com

Distribution Network
gyanbooks.com
India, USA, Canada, UK, Australia

ISBN: 978-93-6208-382-1 (HB)
First Published, 1937

2nd Impression 2024

Printed at: Gyan Press, Delhi.

THE GRAND REBEL
Author: DENNIS KINCAID

THE GRAND REBEL

An Impression of Shivaji
Founder of the Maratha Empire

BY

DENNIS KINCAID

COLLINS
FORTY-EIGHT PALL MALL LONDON
1937

DEDICATION

To DAVID FARRER

MY DEAR DAVID,

As most of this book was written when you and I were in Greece together, I think it should very properly be inscribed to you.

Yours ever,

DENNIS.

"That Grand Rebel Sevagee. . . ."

East India Company Correspondence (*passim*).

"Aurangzebe used to call Sevagi the Mountain Rat; and we have often wondered what affinity there could be to give occasion for his Epithet . . . but we have now found in Brett's Feyjoo a description of the properties of which Feyjoo calls the Rat of India, that makes the appellation applied to Sevaji a compliment and very characteristic of his military policy. However, we must not be sure that Aurangzebe had this animal in his idea, until we know whether it exists in India Proper."

Orme.

CONTENTS

PREFACE

MOST English people have heard of the Moguls as almost the traditional pre-British rulers of India. They then find it puzzling that the earlier heroes of Anglo-Indian biography apparently never oppose any Moguls but are constantly in difficulties with the Marathas. They are perhaps reminded of their readings in Roman history at school when they find the stage occupied permanently by the Romans, to whom enter in turn a number of outlandish characters called Pyrrhus, Mithridates or Jugurtha just in time to receive their *coup de grâce*. What they were doing behind the scenes before responding to their cue is left obscure. Similarly, in the history of India various tribes or kingdoms labelled Marathas only appear for the first time when clearly working up for chastisement. Such of their chiefs who were so unfortunate as to oppose Anglo-Indian celebrities are generally reprobated as rebels; their names, which Victorian writers made earnest but incorrect attempts to spell, provide an easy target for such sprightly historians of to-day as Mr. Guedalla, who are entertained by the un-English sound of them. But just as at school one's curiosity was often piqued less by the inevitable Romans than by their unsuccessful opponents, many people must have vaguely wondered about these Marathas; the rise of whose power was exactly contemporaneous with the appearance of the English in India; who destroyed the Mogul Empire and disputed with both English and French for the mastery of a sub-continent; who once more opposed the English in the Mutiny, providing in Nana Sahib the cleverest and in the Princess of Jhansi the best and bravest, of the revolutionary leaders; and from whom have sprung rulers of such deserved repute as Princess Ahalyabai of Indore and the present Gaekwar of Baroda, and dynasties as devoted to the Empire as Gwalior and Kolhapur.

This book is a study of the founder of the Maratha state whose memory inspired the rise of modern Hindu Nationalism, a man for whom a majority of Hindus entertain much the same sentiment as the Germans for Frederick the Second and the Italians for Garibaldi, and whom the Marathas adore as more than human.

PROLOGUE

THE MARATHAS

THE Marathas are the people who inhabit the triangular province of India known as Maharashtra, the base of the triangle lying upon the seacoast from Daman to Karwar and the apex running inland to Nagpur. This territory is divided from north to south by a range of mountains, the Western Ghats. To the west of these mountains the country is low lying, fertile and damp; to the east it is dry and largely barren, pockets of earth alternating with outcrops of bare rock. The true home of those clansmen who built the Maratha power is in the country just under the eastern shadow of the Ghats, the narrow valleys bounded by spurs of the great hills.

Until the lifetime of Shivaji there was no specifically Maratha state nor any sense of Maratha nationality. The kings of Central and Western India throughout the early and middle ages had their chief towns in the Maratha country, and the people of that country shared in the extraordinary prosperity of Western India in the first three centuries of our era. Trade with Europe was brisk; there were Greek merchants in all the coast towns and Greek mercenaries at the courts of local princes. In the fifth and sixth centuries these princes exchanged envoys with Sassanian Persia and constructed the astounding rock-temples of Ajanta.

But away from the cosmopolitan atmosphere of the courts and the commercial centres, the character of the Maratha people would appear to have been then much the same as it is to-day or was in the time of Shivaji. A Chinese visitor of the seventh century thus described them:—

"Their manners are simple and honest. They are proud and reserved. If any one is kind to them, he can be sure of their gratitude, but if any one injures them they will take their revenge. They will risk their lives to wipe out dishonour. If any one in distress appeals to them, they will lay aside all thought of self in their anxiety to help. Even if they have an insult to avenge, they never fail to warn their enemy. In battle, if they pursue the fugitives they always spare all who surrender. . . . These men love study and there are many heretics among them."

Shortly after this visitor returned home an Arab prince from Irak led an army up the Indus and in 720 annexed the lower Indus province to the Caliphate of Bagdad. It was the first instalment of the Mussulman advance. The Hindu Kingdoms of the north were reduced one by one, the size of India being so great that the various states found it even harder to combine against the Mussulman invader than European nations in the time of Pius II. The earlier supersession of Buddhism with its cosmopolitan culture and international affiliations by the revival of the national religion of Hinduism had led to the cultural isolation of central and southern Indian States. Now the Mussulman conquests broke the trade-links with north and west. The courts of princes in the Maratha country became less showy and more provincial. Marathi began to emerge as a language distinct from its neighbours. 1290 saw the first considerable Marathi work, a translation of the sacred *Gita*. Exactly four years later the Afghan invasion of the Maratha country began. By 1313 the conquest was complete and the Marathas had to wait for three and a half centuries before Shivaji restored to them their independence.

If the Mussulman conquest retarded the emergence of a Maratha state, it welded the Maratha people together in attachment to their religion; which began to centre increasingly round the cult of local saints, followers of Krishna and preachers of salvation through discipline and sacrifice. This religion of the Maratha country has little in common with the estatic and Cybelic cults of some parts of India over which foreign critics have wasted so much virtuous indignation. Nor are even those either characteristic of, or inevitable in, Hinduism; they are only as relevant to an estimate of that faith as the temple-conditions of Corinth to an estimate of the religion of the Greeks. Hinduism is the last remaining branch of the great religion of the Archaic Culture that was the ancestor, through Sumeria and Egypt and Crete, of the western world. Whereas in the West the irruption of the Aryan barbarians disturbed the equilibrium of the Archaic religion by a supersession of gods of forest and cave by sky-gods and hero-gods, in India the Aryan effect was transitory. If the world of the Indian epics resembles that of Homer, the air of a lonely village to-day is, once more, that of the cities of the Indus civilization; the same sense of nature, the cult of the genius loci, the worship of the snake and fertility fetish, the peaceful fatalism, the enormous respect for woman. One must remember that behind the feudal chivalry of the Rajputs, the façade of prosperous courts influenced by the Aryan ideal or by new clan traditions from the steppes, the quiet, intense life of the Hindu village continued in an unbroken tradition from Harappa till now. The Marathas, reacting from their domination by Mongol, Arab and Turk, emerged suddenly as a military people; but they drew their strength from the continuity of deep-founded traditions and from a certain solidity of character which has remained curiously unchanged. The description, quoted above, of a Chinese visitor in the seventh century might well be that of an English visitor to-day.[1]

Indeed, Englishmen and Marathas often discover a great mutual sympathy. The fight for control of India at the end of the eighteenth and beginning of the nineteenth centuries was mainly between these two people. It required three wars to break the Maratha power. Yet you find less resentment and bitterness against the conqueror in those wars among Marathas than perhaps among any other people in India. The services of Maratha princes and Maratha soldiers in the Great War offer some proof of that. When you are wandering in the Maratha hills you chance upon a war memorial in some tiny hamlet; and it is moving to read that, say, eleven men went from that village (probably so small a place that you are surprised that it could send so many able-bodied men to the Army) to serve in Irak. Many of these village lads were at Kut. Very few men, once taken prisoner, returned or were heard of again. The clean-fighting Turk saw to that.

Marathas are generally dark with firm, bronze-coloured flesh. Their figures are square and sturdy. They wear to-day, in their villages, much the same

[1] cf. Bom. Gazetteer XVIII: "They are hard-working, temperate, hospitable, brave, fond of their children and kind to strangers."

dress that their ancestors did a century or two centuries ago, a short divided skirt reaching to the knees and a jacket tied across the chest with coloured tape; a flat turban, generally red; sandals or red shoes, often carried in the hand for economy's sake; and in wet weather a heavy dark cloak enveloping the body and flung over one shoulder. They are fastidious in cleanliness and pride themselves on the orderly neatness of their houses, the well-scrubbed floors, the freshly-plastered walls and the row of polished brass vessels in the kitchen. They are proverbial for their shame of acknowledging poverty. A Maratha who has only one penny left will spend that on butter to smear on his fingers and then sit at the door of his house washing his hands to give his neighbours the impression that he has just dined sumptuously.[1]

Their women are free of speech and notably outspoken; purdah being unknown among them. Indeed the Maratha woman is proverbial for her courage and endurance and for a peculiarly biting wit. She will readily talk even with a stranger or foreigner, but he should beware of her sharpening her wit on him, while her menfolk stand round shaking with merriment; at the same time she will not resent a retort, however sharp, and when the laugh is turned against her she will enjoy the joke at her expense as well as any one. She is seldom of

[1] "Tribes and Castes of the Bombay Presidency." (Bom. Govt. Press.)

striking beauty but her figure is sometimes of extraordinary elegance and symmetry. Her dress, the long Maratha *sari*, folded and worn with traditional care, falls with the grace of a Tanagra figurine's chiton.

The Maratha village centres round the village temple; often an old, finely-carved shrine shaded with silver-grey pipal trees. The houses have generally but one storey; the roofs either thatched or rising steeply like the roofs of a chalet in a wave of red-brown tiles. The woodwork of windows, balconies and doors is often ingeniously, and sometimes beautifully, carved. The house of a rich man (rich, that is, by village standards) may have paintings on its walls; a yellow cobra, a bluish elephant or the youth Krishna playing on his flute.

Most of the day the men will be working in the fields. In the evenings they gather in the forecourt of the temple, sharing a hookah, and exchanging handfuls of cardamum seeds to chew. The Headman reminisces of days when crops were better and rain more plentiful than now; the schoolmaster reads aloud from a crumpled newspaper; and, as evening deepens into night, the village minstrel takes his zither and sings ballads of the national hero, Shivaji.

PART ONE

CHILDHOOD AND YOUTH

CHAPTER ONE

THE family of Shivaji claimed a double descent both from King Porus, and from the Ranas of Udaipur. Porus, it will be remembered, was the Indian King who opposed Alexander. This claim would appear to have been made in the same spirit as the boast of the Julian House of royal Trojan descent. Alexander has always exercised a strange fascination over the imagination of Indians. In Baluchistan to-day stout chieftains with turbans as large as those of ballet-Sultans in a Bakst décor will solemnly assure you that Alexander passed through their village some time last century, adding as if with a real effort to be accurate, "I cannot quite remember him myself. I was only a child." So in the absence of any evidence one cannot but agree with the judicious Mr. Orme in his pronouncement: "The descent of the Chitore Rajahs from Porus, although asserted by European travellers, does not seem to be established."

The claim of relationship with the House of Udaipur has, on the other hand, not been contested except by enemies of Shivaji and appears to have been accepted by contemporaries. The family name of Bhosle is said to be derived from the fief of Bhosavat in Udaipur, whence a prince named Sajansing fled after the first Mussulman conquest of Udaipur to seek his fortune as a soldier of fortune in the south.

As mercenaries the Bhosles settled in the Maratha country, hiring their swords to one or other of the Mussulman princes who ruled there.

In theory all Muhammadan India owed allegiance to the Emperor of Delhi. The dynasties at Delhi changed; Emperors rose from as various races as in the later Roman Empire. But after what I might call the Bull of Sovereignty obtained by Muhammad Tughlak from the Caliph of Bagdad, the Emperor at Delhi was nominally overlord of India. In fact, however, outlying provinces were always more or less independent; and the tyranny of Muhammad Tughlak, the Tsar Paul I., of India, provoked a wide rebellion in southern India where a new dynasty, known as the Bahmani, established itself. The relations between the Bahmani kingdom and the empire were not unlike those between Eastern and Western Europe after the suppression of the Roman principate in Italy. The Basileus might temporarily acquiesce in the usurpation of Ostrogoth and Visigoth in the Western provinces, but a Justinian would seize a favourable opportunity to reassert not only imperial claims but the reality of Imperial power. The throne of Delhi was for two centuries occupied by weak rulers and there were periods of anarchy enlivened by the massacres of Tamerlane.

To this condition the Bahmani kingdom offered as favourable a contrast as Italy under Theodoric to the Balkans under Anastasius. But just as the Gothic kingdoms crumbled away while Byzantium emerged refreshed and vigorous under new strong dynasties, so the Bahmani kingdom broke up into five comparatively weak states—Golconda, Bijapur, Ahmednagar, Berar and Bidar—while the throne of Delhi was, in 1526, occupied by Babar, the first of the great Mogul dynasty. None of the five kingdoms of the south was a match for the military power of the revived Empire. These kingdoms had paused in their mutual hostilities to unite against the last Hindu state of the south, that of Vijayanagar, and to destroy it utterly. In spite, however, of the lengthening shadow of the Great Mogul their unity was short-lived; and while Berar was absorbed in the Empire without serious resistance, Bidar was conquered and annexed by Bijapur. There remained then, three kingdoms: Golconda, Bijapur and Ahmednagar.

Shivaji's grandfather, Maloji, a soldier of fortune like all his ancestors since their flight from Udaipur, chose to offer his sword to the king of Ahmednagar. He was received with favour and married the sister of a prominent courtier. In 1594 Shahaji, Shivaji's father, was born.

At the Ahmednagar court there were many

Maratha officials and chief among them was a wealthy landowner called Lahkoji, who was the leading personage in the Hindu community in the city. On the occasion of any great festival he would throw open his house and grounds to his fellow Hindus. In the spring of 1599 they were celebrating Holi, the Hindu festival of spring, in Lahkoji's house. Dancing-boys with bells at their ankles stamped their feet in time round the courtyard of the house and chanted hymns to the spirits of fertility while trumpets and fifes played cheerfully. The guests chased each other, shouting and laughing and sprinkling coloured water over each other's bright clothes, for such horseplay is traditional at this festival. Generally the children sat solemn-eyed against the carved pillars of the arcade that ran round three sides of the courtyard and wonderingly watched the unusual levity of their parents—an odd departure from the formality and gravity of Hindu life. On this occasion, however, Jijabai, the five-year-old daughter of the host, began to mimic the grown-up guests' high-spirited games and ran about sprinkling people with coloured water. Young Shahaji imitated her and splashed water over the girl's dress of green and white.[1] Soon the two children had drenched each other's clothes. As they stood laughing, bright-eyed and flushed, Lahkoji passed and was moved at their happiness.

[1] The traditional colours of the dresses of women at this festival.

"What a charming couple," he said.

Maloji, ambitious and unscrupulous, at once called the attention of every one present to his host's exclamation, which he interpreted as a proposal to betroth the two children. Such early betrothals (which do not necessarily imply marriage till many years later, or even if the marriage ceremony is performed the couple return to their own homes till they reach a proper age to live together) are common enough in India; and Hindu etiquette is very strict on the fulfilment of all promises of betrothal.

Lahkoji, as the chief Hindu noble at the Ahmednagar court, would not have dreamed of betrothing his daughter to the son of a soldier of fortune. He was appalled at the meaning read into his light words. He tried to laugh the matter off, but next morning Maloji sent him a formal request to confirm his proposal. Lahkoji refused and Maloji, professing indignation at the insult, challenged him to a duel.

The king of Ahmednagar heard of the quarrel. He did not want to lose either Lahkoji, a loyal noble, or Maloji, a capable soldier. So with the amiable caprice of a Sultan he raised Maloji to the command of five thousand horse and gave him a fief. If still unequal in rank and wealth to Lahkoji, Maloji was now at least a person of substance, and, pressed by the king, Lahkoji gave way and allowed his daughter Jijabai to be formally betrothed, and after five or six years married, to young Shabaji. Three or four years later they began to live together and presently Jijabai had a son called Sambhaji.

Shahaji followed his father in the service of Ahmednagar. However, in 1636 that kingdom collapsed and Shahaji enlisted in the armies of Bijapur. His possession of the fief granted to his father was reaffirmed by his new master.

Now of the five original Muhammadan states of South India only Golconda and Bijapur remained, both theoretically feudatories of the Emperor at Delhi, but in practice independent. To translate his nominal overlordship into real authority, the Emperor Shah Jahan, having annexed most of the territories that till recently formed part of the Ahmednagar kingdom, pressed southwards to attack Bijapur.

Shahaji's lands, granted to his father Maloji, lay in the path of the imperial advance. He resisted for a while, and then rode southwards to Bijapur, taking with him his baby son Sambhaji, but abandoning not only his lands but also his wife Jijabai who was again pregnant.

CHAPTER TWO

JIJABAI took refuge in Shivner, a fort in the hill-country. A few faithful retainers manned the half-ruined bastions. Beyond the walls stretched panther-haunted woods and melancholy wastes of jungle and in the mornings when the gates were cautiously opened and a file of women went down through the mist to fill their jars with fresh water from a spring, they would notice the tracks of bears clear in the red soil.

A wild and lonely place and Jijabai must often have contrasted her father's comfortable mansion with the poor cottage where she now lived and the narrow limits of the fort from whose gates you could not venture far for fear of brigands and wild beasts. But there was less to fear here than in the plains below where the armies of the Empire and of Bijapur contended, disputing each mile of that frontier tract. The soldiers of both armies were mercenaries and largely foreigners—Arabs, Pathans, Turks, Afghans and Africans. Their pay often in arrears, they hunted down the Hindu peasantry, destroyed the crops, carried off the cattle and the women and boys, without caring to which ruler their victims professed allegiance. The land went out of cultivation and the surviving peasants became bandits.

Happy in her temporary security, Jijabai prepared for the birth of her child. She was very religious and carefully followed all the Hindu rites prescribed for pregnant women. She drew triangles, adorned with vermilion bosses, on the walls of her cottage and anointed them daily with honey and molasses and melted butter in honour of the Mother-Goddess.[1] While the fort garrison anxiously scanned the line of hills, Jijabai was strangely content. In dreams she heard voices prophesying fame for her child as yet unborn.

She was not the only person in India then exercised by similar premonitions. There were curious rumours in the far south where the memory of Hindu independence was more recent and the hope of a Hindu revival not yet dead. India has always been notable for the mysterious way in which rumours and warnings travel with lightning-like rapidity from village to village—the *chapatti* messages just before the Mutiny will be remembered. And a few months before Shivaji's birth an odd prophecy was repeated in the villages of the south, a Sanskrit verse, "The time of deliverance is at hand. Maidens herald it with songs of joy and the heavens shower blossoms on the earth. . . ."[2]

[1] For these rites, see Enthoven, *Folklore of the Bombay Presidency.* (O.U.P.)

[2] Wilkes: *Mysore.* Ranad.

On April 16th, 1627, Jijabai gave birth to a second son whom she called Shivaji. The ceremonies at the birth of a Hindu man-child are as numerous as at all other occasions in the drama of Hindu life; but the chief actor in them is the father. But the father, who should have been standing by the couch of Jijabai and her son, was far away. The room, darkened with drawn shutters, must have grown hot with the purifying fires in whose uncertain light the watching faces of priests were sometimes startlingly clear and sometimes veiled in gloom, and as Jijabai lay silent and at rest after the pain, she perhaps felt with new sorrow the absence of her husband and her helpless loneliness. Some other man must have deputised for Shahaji, and, in accordance with Hindu ritual, laid the man-child in a winnowing fan, kissed its head in blessing and let honey fall through a gold ring upon the child's mouth.[1]

Some time after the birth ceremonies come what (there being no European equivalent) I might call the profession-testing. The child is laid on a carpet and before him are spread symbols of the various professions—a pen for a clerk, a sword for a soldier and so forth—so that the child, by pointing to one or other of these symbols may indicate what profession his parents should prepare him for. One can hazard the guess that Shivaji's fingers strayed in

[1] These ceremonies from the chapter "Customs of the Higher Castes in Maharashtra" in Kincaid and Parasnis' *History of the Maratha People.*

the direction of the sword, even if the discreet pressure of a priest's hand never urged him (as so often happens at such ceremonies) towards the symbol of that occupation which would be seemly for the child's rank and caste.

Meanwhile the Mogul commander was still searching for Shahaji, for till the local landowners had been rounded up and forced into formal submission to the Emperor the district could not be considered properly conquered. But when it was learnt that Shahaji had left the district and was safe in Bijapur city, they began to hunt for his wife and child.

The earliest words that Shivaji heard must have been of anxiety and fear, for the fort where his mother had taken refuge could never stand a regular siege, and the only hope was that the Mogul patrols might not know where Jijabai was. A childhood passed in alternating alarm and relief. . . .

And then when Shivaji was six the blow fell. We do not know whether the secret of Jijabai's hiding-place was betrayed to the Moguls by some tribesman corrupted by a bribe, or whether they learnt of her refuge by chance. All we know is that while Jijabai was captured the Moguls never found Shivaji. Perhaps the alarm was given in time for a servant to snatch up the child and dart from the back gates of the fort into the jungle, while Jijabai gained time by arguing with her captors.

The Mogul headquarters were then at Trimbak, a spot especially holy to Hindus, for in the vast black cliff that overhangs the town is a spring where the sacred Godavari rises. To-day it is an enchanting place; black stone temples of a simple grandeur; jacaranda trees blooming in temple courtyards; a stream, running down the main street of the town, overhung with trees and crossed by high carved bridges. But when Jijabai came in a palanquin surrounded by Mogul troopers through the wide-thrown gates of the town, the houses were in ruins and the streets empty. Jijabai must have felt her heart wither in despair; they had caught her; they must inevitably find her son.

The Mogul commander was more humane than many; but his humanity was born of indifference. Jijabai's only value to him would have been as a hostage; and perhaps he knew that Shahaji, away in Bijapur, had taken another wife. But the child was another matter; capture the son and the father would come to heel. He ordered the patrols in the hills to redouble their efforts. Jijabai was sent under guard to a fortress.

For three years devoted servants carried Shivaji with them in the recesses of the hills, pursued by the Moguls. Even to-day these hills are a wild labyrinth of narrow passes between huge cliffs where the air is stifling and damp; of rolling uplands where the yellow speargrass stabs one's ankles and the leafless shrubs seems to crouch, tightly gripping the shallow pebble-strewn soil; of endless avenues through the luxuriant forest, under one's feet a carpet of rotting leaves squelching at every step, and all round the suspense of breathless noon. Bitter the winter in those hills, a thick mist clinging about the trees almost till noon, so that even the hillmen come out into the daylight like chill, numbed flies, slowly stretching their aching limbs in the sun. . . . In May come the long rains. At first a few showers, pleasant after parching drought. A thick mist in the ravines, while in the darkening woods the coppersmith bird hoots menacingly in warning of the approaching storm. Red clouds climbing the sky; a hush and sense of tension; and then with the first outburst of thunder, trees bend and scream under a sea-bitter wind, and the rain falls in hard white rods that beat the grass flat and send rocks hurtling down precipices and sound upon cottage roofs like the clamour of kettledrums.

Through winter and monsoon and short, breathless summer the fugitives wandered in the hills, never daring to rest long under any roof, always in constant anxiety. It would be difficult to exaggerate the effect on the child's mind of these three years. While most well-to-do Hindus had come to accept Muslim domination as inevitable and had been seduced by the luxury and comfort of Muhammadan courts, Shivaji spent his earlier childhood among men not yet subdued, among wild tribesmen and in lonely forest villages. Other young Hindus of his rank lived as neighbours with Muhammadan gentry and if they were despised and sometimes persecuted, they accepted such inconveniences without too much complaint; but to Shivaji the Muhammadans were the people who had taken his mother away and who followed him relentlessly, the ogres of his childhood.

When he was ten his mother escaped from her fortress, but we do not know any details of the manner of her escape. She joined her son in the hills. She can hardly have hoped to see him again. In the loneliness of her imprisonment she had turned increasingly to religion for comfort; and the reunion with her son must have seemed almost a miraculous answer to her prayers. The war between the Empire and Bijapur was drawing wearily to its end and the Moguls abandoned their search for Shivaji. Glad of the respite, mother and son lived together in some cottage in the hills. Shivaji never forgot listening to his mother, while she told him of the old glories of Hinduism and how her family and his father's had been free and noble even before the coming of the Greeks, in days when Hindustan was the land of the Hindus indeed.

Meanwhile envoys passed between Delhi and

Bijapur. The Emperor Shah Jahan—finding in his old age greater pleasure in music and in graceful dancers than in the dreary details of campaigns—was weary of the war. His secretaries wrote letters couched in the proper terms of Persian diplomacy to the Sultan of Bijapur addressing him for a whole page with titles such as "Sun of the Sky of State, Gem and Mirror of Purity, Asylum of Grandeur, the Great Lord to whom the angelic mind of His Majesty the Emperor is very attentive," and in the end referring to him as Khan, or Nobleman, but never as Sultan or King.[1] The Sultan replied with suitable humility, calling the Emperor the "Protector of the world, Vice-regent of God, Lord of Felicity, O Solomon . . ." The Mogul sent the Sultan a present of a horse and there was an enraptured acknowledgment. "This horse, a moon in beauty, treads the heaven like the imagination of an astronomer. Over his haunches is a saddle-cloth of Turkish velvet. He is a true Persian. He wanders in the woods like Majnun; his tail is more lovely than the locks of Laila."

When yet another letter arrived from the Emperor, the Sultan placed it respectfully on his head and professed to have been inspired by the very touch of it. "I became so exalted that I can hope for nothing better."

[1] These letters may be read in the *Archæological Survey of India*, Vol. XXXVII., under "Bijapur Sanads."

The end of all those elegant exchanges was a treaty in 1637 by the terms of which the Sultan acknowledged Shah Jahan as suzerain and agreed to pay tribute. The boundary between the Empire and Bijapur was drawn just north of that tract of land which had been granted to Shivaji's grandfather Maloji.

As soon as the war was over, Shahaji sent to call his son and wife to Bijapur. So for the first time Shivaji left the hill country where he had spent his vagabond childhood. It must have been a melancholy journey, through districts ruined by the war; burnt villages and crumbling towns; temples deliberately defaced and defiled; a few trees, smoke-blackened and stunted; and then miles and miles of empty uninhabited land, rolling yellow downs, ochre spear-grass sighing in the wind. It was only as they approached Bijapur City that they came upon evidence of life and prosperity. Here there were gardens and canals and orchards and white mosques in groves of mango. And lifting their eyes the travellers would have seen in the distance a line of domes and towers along the sky; Bijapur, the Indian Palmyra.

CHAPTER THREE

PROBABLY the first thing that struck a visitor to Bijapur was the symbol of the crescent which was displayed on every public building. He would learn that this was the family crest of the dynasty of Bijapur who boasted relationship with the Caliphs at Constantinople, and so had mimicked them in the use of the crescent.[1] Since the other Mussulman rulers in India, from the Emperor downwards, were of Indo-Persian or Central Asian descent, this solitary ruling family of Ottoman blood is interesting and worth a short digression on its origins.

The Osmanli, Bayezid the Thunderbolt, proclaimed Sultan[2] on the field of Kossovo, fatal to Serbia, had ordered the execution of his younger brother to avoid even the possibility of a rival. From this single savage impulse arose the precedent followed at the proclamation of each succeeding Turkish Sultan. All royal princes, except the heir,

[1] Which, of course, has nothing to do with Islam and was, like everything else popularly considered distinctively Turkish, borrowed from the Greeks. The crescent had been the city crest of Byzantium from the time of the siege by Philip II., when the moon suddenly appearing from behind a cloud warned the sentries of an impending assault.

[2] Not Caliph. The Caliphate was only assumed after Selim's conquest of Egypt.

were slaughtered so that no dynastic feuds should disturb the new reign. In 1451, Muhammad II., to become known as the Conqueror, decreed on his accession the usual massacre. His youngest brother, a child called Yusuf, was the favourite son of their mother. She begged from the new Sultan a day's respite for Yusuf. This was granted. It happened that a merchant called Gargastani was then at the court disposing of Georgian slaves. The Sultana sent for Gargastani by night, bought from him a Georgian lad of the same age as her son and handed over Yusuf to him with a sum of money in return for his promise to bring up the young prince in his own home. Then she caused the Georgian slave to be strangled and when the executioners came at dawn she showed them the corpse of a boy and pretended it was that of her son whom she had preferred to have killed rather than relinquish to the common executioners. Whether she added to her explanations a bribe or whether the executioners were tired of their work, this not very probable story was accepted and the body of the Georgian changeling was taken in funeral pomp through the city.

Meanwhile the merchant Gargastrini returned to his house in Saveh with the young prince. Had the Sultana remained content with her ruse we should never have heard of the story and Yusuf would have grown up in Saveh as apprentice to his master, ending perhaps as a prosperous slave dealer like him.

But his mother could not forget him and once a year she sent a messenger to Saveh for news about her son. In an Oriental court no one's secrets are safe. Soon there were whispers about the Sultana's unaccountable interest in a remote town. The Governor of Saveh was told to inquire. Yusuf, warned in time, fled eastwards through Persia to India which he reached in 1459. Penniless and friendless, he was trapped by a slave dealer and sold to a noble in Central India, Mahmud Gavan. A clever, handsome boy, he soon gained his master's favour and presently Mahmud Gavan adopted him as his son.

Now, Mahmud Gavan was an officer in the service of the Bahmani king, who, it will be remembered, ruled over Central India. One day he fell into disfavour and the king ordered his execution. He was duly beheaded, but Yusuf, escaping from the court, appealed to the regiments which Mahmud Gavan had commanded. They acclaimed him as Mahmud's heir and offered to march against the king. At the head of an army, Yusuf extorted from the king the governorship of Bijapur. Governor and soon independent prince, he founded for himself a kingdom. His successors built and beautified their capital till it became one of the most splendid cities in Asia.[1]

[1] For the history of Bijapur, Cousens' *Bijapur* and *Arch. Survey of India*, Vol. 37.

You must imagine Shivaji's awe as he rode in under the great north gate over which ran the proud inscription, "The Sultan,[1] whose orders are current in the seven regions, has erected a rampart worthy of Alexander," and stared up at the gigantic walls and bastions, which even to-day in their ruin are of Cyclopean proportions. Along the walls were the guns for which the city was famous, for it rulers had brought with them a Turkish interest and skill in artillery. Fantastic in design and adorned with precious stones, these guns were treated as though they were fetishes. Troops on the march saluted them and they were protected from the sun by umbrellas of state. Greatest of all the guns was one called Malik-i-Maidan, which means Monarch of the Plain. It had been constructed by the famous artillerist Khan Murad who caused to be cut on one side the inscription, phrased as though in answer to a challenge, "Hast thou tried me, O Apostle of Allah?"; and on the other the more complacent "I have subdued this monarch." Its muzzle was so big that a man could sit inside. It was fashioned like the head of a dragon with open jaws and fangs bared. The ears of the dragon were drilled for the insertion of ear-rings. This gun was held in such esteem that the Sultan kept it covered with cloth of gold and once a year came in solemn

[1] The ruler of Bijapur's official title was Sultan, which has not to Indians the same august ring as to Europeans, who usually associate it with the Ottoman ruler. Sultan only means king.

procession to do it reverence.[1] Even to-day, its trappings and adornments gone, lying along the ruined walls like a stranded whale, it is worshipped by the people, who smear it with red lead and scented oil, hang garlands about its neck and bowing before the monstrous jaws, offer upon brass trays handfuls of rose petals.

Passing through the gateway Shivaji and his mother must have gazed at the mosques and palaces and tombs. There was the Gol Gumbaz with its honey-coloured dome, the largest dome in the world,[2] its walls covered with lapiz lazuli inscribed in great gold letters with, "The tomb of Sultan Muhammad whose abode is in Paradise." And there was the Ibrahim Rauja, more lovely than all the white Mogul buildings of the north, with its slim minarets from which hung an incredible number of stone chains as delicately carved as silver filigree work, clanking together in the warm wind. All round the building were gardens with groves of blossoming trees and rivulets of cold clear water sighing down channels of coloured marble. In the gloom, under the dome that was like an opal bubble, were the tombs of the Sultans and their wives. A man's grave would have on it a large white pen-case to show that the man had been scholarly in his lifetime, for this quality was considered estimable

[1] Pietro della Valle, *Travels*, London Hakluyt Society, Vol. I.
[2] The next largest is that of the Pantheon at Rome.

in a man, but not in a woman. The women's graves were flat-topped with flattering epitaphs written on them. That of Queen Taj Sultana, for whom the mausoleum had been originally raised, read, "Dignified and exalted as Solomon's Queen Bilkis, kindly and affable, the very diadem of modesty, when she left this realm she ascended to heaven." And over the north door under the fan of the most delicately-carved marble, the architect Malik Sandal had written, with a certain lack of modesty, "Heaven stood astounded at this building. The garden of Paradise has borrowed its beauty from this garden and every column here is as graceful as the cypress trees in the garden of purity. An angel from heaven cried out, 'This building which rejoices the heart is a fitting memorial to Queen Taj Sultana.'"

Perhaps the most astonishing building of all was the Palace of the Relic, an edifice raised to house a silver casket in which were two hairs of the Prophet Muhammad. Italian artists had been chartered by the Sultan to cover the walls with bright frescoes. It will be remembered how stern is the Islamic ban on all representations of the human form; but such old-fashioned superstitions did not concern the dilettante Sultan. Strange, and to the orthodox Muslim North most horrifying, were the subjects these Italian painters chose. They painted scenes at a dinner party where the women sat crowned with flowers eating fruit from dishes of Venetian glass while slave girls played on organs, violas and harps. They painted European gentlemen in wide hats and lace collars with dogs at their heels. And here was a Venus, rose-crowned, with pearls at her neck, a plump Veronese figure leaning back languidly while Cupid, with blue wings, a jewelled belt, bracelets and pearl earrings, held a mirror before her face. Mars, a winged helmet in one hand, raised his other hand in amorous appeal to the queen of love. In a garden Venus sported with Adonis. A Persian musician recited poetry to a group of ladies, some European and some Oriental; he rolled his head to attract attention but the ladies chattered happily together, ignoring him.[1]

In most quarters of the town were public baths—for the dynasty had brought from Brusa and Nicæa Byzantine conceptions of luxury. There was one open-air bathing pool and over the gateway was this inscription, "A lovely pool! Its water is bright and pure, clearer than a well in Paradise, sweeter than rose-water, its every bubble like the moon."[2] Other baths were covered, the walls lined with chunam, fluted and painted, the vaulted domes powdered with mother-of-pearl. And down all the main streets were fountains for the poor to drink at. Their inscriptions still remain: "The glorious and

[1] Full details of these paintings appear in Griffith's Report, 1884, quoted in Arch. Survey of India, Vol. XXXVII., pp. 93-94.

[2] *Bombay Gazetteer*, Vol. XXIII.

powerful Sultan, whose court is as gorgeous as Solomon's, has made this fountain in order that the thirsty may drink therefrom and may then keep their tongues swift with prayers for the ever-enduring reign of the Sultan, who is the asylum of the universe."

Luxury, refinement and buildings of exquisite art—but in few kingdoms have violent deaths been more frequent. Processions of execution were as frequent as processions of holiday and festival. Under the famous Baobab Tree,[1] fifty feet in girth, bare of foliage, with gaunt gnarled branches and bloated trunk, Abyssinian executioners awaited their victims. When the condemned men approached the Abyssinians salaamed to them before unsheathing their heavy swords[2] . . . The nobles who passed Shivaji in the thronged streets, their retainers thrusting aside his mother's shabby palanquin, their kettledrums and gold-fringed umbrellas advertising the approach of a person of consequence—these nobles lived lives of tension and suspense, uneasy at each rumour and suspicious of each other. There were bitter discussions even in the palace, and disputes between the courtiers often assumed the

[1] It is still standing, and is, perhaps naturally, believed to be haunted, not only by Indians, but also by Europeans, many of whom tell apparently well-attested stories of unpleasant manifestations.

[2] Cousens' *Bijapur*. Abyssinians were widely employed in India. Most were Muhammadans, but there were a few Christians, remarkable for the great cross that they had burnt on their faces, stretching from forehead to chin and ear to ear (Linschoten, *Voyage aux Indes*).

conditions of civil war; and all were subject to the caprice of the Sultan or of that one of his ever-changing ministers who for the moment was in favour.

One of these nobles was Shivaji's father, Shahaji. He had prospered as a soldier in Bijapur service and seems to have lost all interest in his lands near the Mogul border. A handsome man, but florid and stout; in his fine Durbar robes only distinguishable as a Hindu by the red caste mark on his forehead. He was contented enough with his place in the hierarchy of Bijapur officialdom and if the Muhammadan courtiers often intrigued against him he had been able so far to rely on the Sultan's favour. He had married a second wife, a younger woman than Jijabai, and one more suited than she to his temperament. By her he had a son named Vyankoji of whom we shall not hear again till the end of Shivaji's life. This second marriage should not, according to Hindu ideas, have greatly embittered Jijabai, nor offered any excuse to Shahaji to treat her with any diminished respect and affection. But it seems clear that Shahaji had never loved Jijabai; a sudden childish impulse, and his father's quick ambition—these had brought Shahaji into a loveless marriage, and he seems to have felt an increasing aversion to Jijabai. Now after several years of separation he must have found her even more out of sympathy with him than when they first lived together, so hardened had her character become. She was no longer beautiful, she was embittered by her trials, she did not conceal her disquiet and disease in the enervating atmosphere of the Islamic city.

Shahaji had not summoned her to Bijapur for the sake of her company, but so that she could bring his son with her. He felt responsible for the boy's upbringing and wanted him to have a suitable career in the Bijapur service where his own influence could ensure him proper advancement. Moreover, there was his marriage to be arranged. At once Jijabai protested that she would not consent to her son's marriage in Bijapur, "lest Muslims defile the ceremony by their presence." Mother and father struggled for their son's allegiance. But Shivaji could not be separated from his mother. He hardly knew his father, and all the rigid Hindu tradition of unquestioning obedience to the head of the family counted for nothing against the memory of his mother's devotion to him, of her loneliness and her capture by the Moguls, and his father's abandonment of her.

Shahaji was torn between two feelings for his precocious, stubborn son. He admired the extraordinary intelligence of the boy—for we are told that Shivaji, instead of playing with other children, would pester his father with questions about affairs of state, methods of administration, and the management of armies. At the same time he was exasperated by Shivaji's disrespect for Muhammadan authorities. For instance, there was his behaviour at the Durbar. Shahaji took his son to pay his respects to the Sultan, as the first move in introducing him into the life of the Court. They entered the great gate of the palace and passed through the outer courts. Here was an edifice known as the Water Pavilion, a tall tower rising from a pool, with balconies made of fretted wood and five-light projecting windows and a parapet of carved lotus petals; the courtiers sat on these balconies on warm evenings and were refreshed by the spray of water spouting from dolphin-shaped pipes and falling in silver rain upon the pool below. Along the walls of the palace were paintings of various Bijapur notables, especially of Muhammad, the sixth Sultan. He was represented reclining on a couch with his favourite dancing girl. Beside him were a basket of flowers, a lute and a Persian book. The portrait was very lifelike and the long-dead prince seemed to smile and nod.[1] Within the Durbar hall the Sultan of Bijapur sat on a low throne, one leg crossed under him, the other outstretched with foot resting on a globe. In one hand he held a gold key, in the other a sword. He wore an embroidered mitre and a Tartar coat, frogged and brocaded, and high boots painted with

[1] Journal of the Bombay Branch of the Royal Asiatic Society, Vol. I., p. 375.

convolvulus flowers.[1] An enormous umbrella of state was held over his head; courtiers wielded gold-handled flywhisks; and on either side of the throne leaf-shaped fans rose and fell. As the courtiers in turn approached the throne they prostrated themselves, bowing their turbans to the carpet. Shahaji followed their example. But his young son, without bowing, saluted the Sultan with the Maratha salaam such as he had seen his own people greet their superiors with in villages of the hill country—the simple manly gesture of raising both hands, with palms together to the level of the chin. What at first the scandalised courtiers took to be the gaucherie of a rustic turned out to be a piece of obstinate defiance. Shivaji could not be persuaded to approach the Sultan's throne in the prescribed manner and it is said that only the high favour which his father then enjoyed at court saved Shivaji from immediate punishment.

After this regrettable incident Shahaji began to lose interest in the child. It was clear he would never be a success at Court. He seemed to have inherited more than a fair share of his mother's character. So Shivaji was left more and more to himself and to his mother. I suppose that if Shahaji had taken a little more trouble over his son and had set himself to influence him through affection and sympathy—

[1] These details are taken from the Adil-Shahi miniature in Lange's *Monuments de Hindustan.*

and, perhaps even more, if he had been fully reconciled with Jijabai and shown her the consideration that was her due—then Shivaji would probably have surrendered in time to the charm of the feudal life of Bijapur and settled down in it happily enough, gradually forgetting his childhood and his earliest impressions. His brother Sambhaji, four years older than Shivaji, having lived in Bijapur while Shivaji and his mother were hiding in the hills, seems to have had no other ambition than loyally to serve the Bijapur government. He entered the Sultan's army and met his death some years later in an obscure skirmish in the far south. But Shahaji seems to have soon lost patience with Shivaji and the boy wandered alone about the city, the bright, country-trained eyes picking out all the details of the life around him; the streets devoted to luxury trades, perfumiers, barbers, painters; the brass-workers hammering out the great vessels for which Bijapur was famous, working naked to the waist, the sun gleaming on the purple-brown backs, while a tame gazelle (the usual pet of the brass workers' guild) ran delicately between their ranks; the rest-houses for the free accommodation of travellers, so luxuriously appointed that men said of them, "to rest therein was for the weary to taste the medicine of felicity."[1] There were European merchants in those rest-houses and Shivaji, who in later life

[1] *Arch. Survey of India*, Vol. XXXVII.

showed so eager a curiosity about the West, must have looked with interest at the foreigners in their strange attire, their wigs, the feathers in their wide hats, their slashed silk clothes and heavy-heeled shoes. But these foreigners for all their fine clothes were easily outshone by the nobles of Bijapur who rode past Shivaji, having "adorned their Elephants, Horses and Lances with Silver Bells and Feathers, Gallant and Rich in Apparel and Sumbrero's. . . . They will miss of a Booty rather than a Dinner; must mount in state and have their Arms carried before them and their Women not far behind them, with the Masters of Mirth and jollity."[1] Nor were these only soldiers and courtiers, for even the merchants "imitate a noble Pomp and are not encountered abroad *nisi magna Comitante caterva*, without a great Train, using many Odors, in the Hummums or Balneos; nor are they without Oils, Perfumes, and Essences of Sandal, Cloves and Oranges which are in their kind very exquisitely drawn off. They go rich in apparel, their Turbats of Gold, Damask'd gold Atlas coats to their heels, embroidered sashes and slippers, Silver and Gold Capparisons on their Horses which are of Arabia, Persia or Turkey."[2] Jostling the trains of merchants and officials were bands of wild Fakirs "wearing a patch'd coat of a saffron colour, with a pretended careless neglect of the World and no certain

[1] Fryer's Account of India, Letter IV. [2] Fryer.

Residence . . . of this Order are many the most Dissolute, Licentious and Prohpane Persons in the World, committing Sodomy, will be Drunk with Bang and Curse God and Mahomet . . . but under this Disguise many pass as Spies up and down and reap the best intelligence for the benefit of the Prince that Employs them."[1]

Behind the splendid façade of the City's life, the display of the courtiers "Insolent and stubborn and not easily Bridled," and the apparently universal reverence shown to the Sultan who was "as *Cæsar* to the *Romans* or *Pharaoh* to the *Egyptians*,"[2] there was a darker side to life in Bijapur. Apart from the violent tenor of life inevitable in such a society, it was obvious that the majority of the Sultan's Hindu subjects were oppressed, intermittently but irritatingly. Even if Fryer's comment that "The Moormen domineer over the Indians (Hindus) most insufferably" were an exaggeration, it seems clear that, with the exception of a few nobles like Shahaji who were happy in high office, the mass of Hindus were made to feel they were an inferior race. But they had long acquiesced in this, and had even grown resigned to the parade of Muhammadan customs that should be abhorrent to Hindus. So there was all the greater astonishment at the news that young Shivaji had made a public protest against cow-slaughter, which was the occasion for

[1] Fryer. [2] *Idem.*

a riot in which the Muhammadan butchers were attacked.

Shivaji again!—Shahaji felt his own position compromised by the boy's defiant behaviour. He ordered Jijabai to take Shivaji away from Bijapur and to return to their ancestral estates on the Mogul frontier. If Shivaji looked back at the palaces and temples of the city it cannot have been with great regret. He was never happier than when alone with his mother and his stay in Bijapur can hardly have provided him with many happy memories.

He only returned to Bijapur the year before his death and then in very different circumstances.

CHAPTER FOUR

IT is not uncommon for a strong new power to rise on the frontier districts between two large but decrepit states. An obvious instance is the sudden emergence of the Ottomans on the border country between the Byzantine Empire and the Seljuk emirates. Nor is it uncommon for the large states to be ruined, less by any positive superiority of the new power rising between them than by their mutually destructive animosity. The success of the Arabs against both Persian and Roman Empires is a case in point. So it is necessary to emphasise the geographical situation of Shivaji's family estates on the very borders of both Bijapur and the Mogul dominions—for this strip of land, given to Shivaji's grandfather by a Muhammadan prince in a gesture reminiscent of the Arabian Nights, was in fact to prove the core of a new empire.

When the Bijapur authorities learned that Shahaji's troublesome son had been sent so far away they must have been relieved; at such a distance nothing that the lad did could be of much importance and anyway he would be properly chastised by the military officers of the border country. It could not have occurred to them that, in certain circumstances, his very distance from Bijapur was an advantage to him. Then there was his proximity to the Mogul border. No help could be expected from the Imperial forces; for in spite of treaties and affirmations of alliance there was little sympathy between the Puritan unifying North and Bijapur with its Shi'a Sultans, its dilettantism and un-Islamic observances, its recurrent pretensions to independent sovereignty.

But at the time of Shivaji's return from Bijapur all such considerations would have appeared fantastic. So far from causing trouble to any government it seemed improbable that Shivaji and his mother would be able to live on their lands. These lands, crossed and recrossed by armies of mercenaries, had been reduced to a wilderness. Most of the villages had disappeared and there were few fields left in cultivation and fewer men to cultivate them. Ruined and desperate, many of the peasants had become brigands and raided the occasional caravans that came that way. Following the ravages of armies had come the famine of 1631–32, one of the most terrible that western India had yet experienced. And as men declined in numbers the wild beasts increased. Wolves became an intolerable scourge. They invaded villages in packs and the starving peasants were almost helpless against them.

Shivaji was now thirteen. His father had appointed

as his tutor and steward a Brahman of that district called Dadaji Kondadev. To many English people there is something faintly sinister about the word Brahman. It suggests priestcraft, obscurantism and subtlety. And certain visitors to India have in their subsequent travel books attributed to the Brahman caste a variety of unattractive qualities. But those who have known intimately, and lived with, Brahman families, would certainly agree that, whatever their faults, the Brahmans of western India impress one as scholarly and courteous, devoted and most loyal friends, their family life of a singular sweetness, yet disciplined by rigid attachment to their exacting faith; grave, lean men, with long heads and light-coloured eyes; their women of extreme grace and often great beauty. Of the Brahman aristocracy Shivaji's tutor was a fine example. His devotion has become proverbial. His one passion was the service of his young master. He was punctilious almost to eccentricity in his honesty. In illustration of this the following story is told. He had caused an orchard to be planted on Shivaji's estate and he warned the servants that any one who stole fruit from the trees would be punished. One day he himself was standing in the orchard at noon; he was thirsty and without thinking he stretched out his hand and picked a ripe mango which swung tantalisingly before him. A moment later he remembered the warning he had addressed to the servants. He fell into an agony of remorse, imagining that people would say that he was as ready to see that other people kept their hands off his master's property as he was to use it for his own purposes. He called for a sword and prepared to hack off the offending hand. The servants crowded round him and, weeping, tried to dissuade him from so extravagant a self-punishment. Even though he laid his sword aside, he wore hereafter a coat without a sleeve for his right arm. If this action, so often quoted in India, sounds affected and theatrical to English readers, it should be remembered that in medieval Europe—where the tenor of life was as melodramatic and the emotional atmosphere as highly-charged as in Mogul India—such a gesture of remorse and penitence would have been neither strange nor unusual.

Dadaji was not only a saint and scholar—he was also a capable administrator. He devoted himself to restoring the estate to something of its former prosperity. He started with the wolf plague, offering a reward from his own savings for each wolf killed. The hillmen found wolf-killing more paying than raids on an occasional caravan, and soon cleared the country of wolves. Then Dadaji tried to tempt back to their fields the peasants, who had fled to the woods and to a life of banditry. He offered good land to them at graded rates—a nominal rental of one rupee for the first year, three rupees for the second, and so up to twenty rupees in the sixth year. Many of the tribesmen of the hills were attracted by this offer, left their forests and mountain villages and settled down in Shivaji's estate, to become in time his enthusiastic adherents. Dadaji recruited other hillmen as armed guards to protect the countryside from brigands.

For the first time for many years the villagers knew relief from constant peril. Confidence returned. Houses began to be rebuilt and in temples were whispered grateful prayers.

The chief village in Shivaji's lands was Puna. Spelled Poona, this place has attained fame as the *locus classicus* of Anglo-Indian yarns. But one must dismiss all such preconceptions and realise that three hundred years ago Poona was a small village, known only for its temples and the orthodoxy of their priests. At the time of Shivaji's return from Bijapur even these temples were in ruins. The village had several times been looted and was now entirely deserted, save by a few fisherfolk who lived along the River Muta. When the last Muhammadan force had passed that way, the commander caused all the houses and walls to be pulled down, and with a final gesture of resentful contempt, ordered a team of asses to be harnessed to a plough and driven over the foundations. Then, solemnly cursing the site of the Hindu town, he planted an iron rod in the earth as a symbol of his malediction.

Dadaji now dug up this iron rod and threw it away. But he realised that the memory of the curse would remain with the superstitious villagers, so he replied to the gesture of the Muhammadan commander by one that was even more dramatic; he had the site ploughed over once again, but this time with white oxen drawing a plough of pure gold.

From a site deserted and shunned, Poona became rapidly a prosperous town. One day it would be the Antioch of Hindu India. To measure the change one may look forward to the days of its splendour and quote the impression of an English visitor, Robertson: "Vast wealth poured into Poona from many causes, the intrigues of foreign powers and the deference shown to the Peshwa or Chief Minister by the Maratha leaders. The city was bright with armed men, handsome horses, rich palanquins and gorgeous houses; messengers ran from place to place; all was gay with sport, dances and merrymaking." But in spite of its wealth and frequent holidays and festivals, Poona was known for its peaceful orderly life. Foreigners remarked on the sensible, sober character of the people. Even in the last decade of Maratha independence, a period clouded by increasing anarchy and confusion, Elphinstone, the last British minister to the Maratha government, wrote of Poona: "On the whole, murders and robberies attended with violence and alarm were very rare, and I have never heard any complaints of the insecurity of property."

Dadaji could not foresee that the little village for whose prosperity he did so much would one day be the capital of India, but it was his patient administration that laid the foundations of Poona's greatness. He raised on the bank of the river a mansion for Shivaji and his mother. They called it the Rang Mahal, or Painted Palace. A Maratha house is generally built round two courtyards; the front courtyard, having a pillared colonnade round it with an archway to the street, is used for the reception of strangers and the recreation of the men of the household; the back courtyard, used generally by the women, has an altar in the centre planted with sacred basil. In the front colonnade the men will recline in the evenings. Servants bring oil lamps, the company rising to salute with lifted hands the yellow flames which are thought to be a symbol of life. This must have been the happiest moment of the day for Dadaji—rest after long hours wrestling with the business of the estate—rest and leisurely perusal of his scrolls of Sanskrit verse—the quiet of evening, the soft lamplight, the black squat Sanskrit characters opening up worlds of beauty. Presently he would call Shivaji and the boy squatted down beside him while he recited the sonorous couplets of old epics, telling of the heroes of Hindustan. And Shivaji sat entranced, while the lamp flames quivered in the night wind, and great moths tumbled about the carved pillars of the colonnade, and the dreams that had haunted him from his earliest childhood became fixed in a passionate ambition. When still only fifteen, he had a seal prepared for himself with this inscription: "Although the first moon is small, men know that it will grow great. This seal befits Shivaji."[1]

As though to prepare himself for the long ordeal of his life, Shivaji spent his days in arduous exercise. He gathered round him a band of hillmen, and with them wandered over the same hills where he had spent those perilous years of his childhood. In the ravines where he had then stumbled wearily he now strode as master. He loved, as all his life, to subject himself to every strain, to test his strength to the utmost. He followed lonely paths where even his companions hesitated to follow; he scrambled along the rocky ledges of sheer cliffs, sending eagles and yellow vultures screaming from their nests. In time he came to know every mile of that wild hill-country as familiarly as his own house in Poona. And the hillmen, at first peering distrustfully from their stockaded villages at

[1] Rajwade. Quoted in Kincaid and Parasnis' *History of the Maratha People*.

rumours of a stranger, presently came to greet him with admiration. He had a smile for all of them; and we know from all who recorded their impressions of him how attractive his smile was. These hillmen were one day to form the backbone of the Maratha army.

After a long day in the forests Shivaji would return to Poona, the hills violet behind him, and before him the rolling yellow fields. As every Hindu does, he would go first to his mother on returning to the house. At that hour she would be worshipping Vishnu before the altar in the centre of the inner courtyard. The altar was planted with sacred basil. She walked slowly round the altar, a lamp in her hand, a golden petal of lamplight in the gathering darkness. When her prayers were over she would talk with Shivaji. They were so much together that they understood each other like lovers.

Presently he would leave her for his supper, for in a Hindu family the men and women eat apart. His supper—a little salted rice and milk, or a few maize-cakes—would be served in the colonnade of the front courtyard, Shivaji reclining against a column, the little pile of rice set on a plantain leaf before him, and all round the leaf the maid servants had drawn designs in coloured chalk.

And after supper his studies with Dadaji. . . .

So the years passed, and Shivaji grew to manhood.

He was by European standards short, but he was broad and very strongly built. His arms were unusually long. He let his beard and moustache grow, and from under his turban a lock of curled hair hung down one side of his face. His eyes were very fine, and contrasted in their soft and melancholy beauty with the curved aquiline nose. The Frenchman, Thevenot, wrote of him: "*Ce rajah est petit et bazané, avec des yeux vifs qui marquent beaucoup d'esprit.*" The English chaplain of Bombay described him as "erect, and of an excellent proportion, active in exercise, and whenever he speaks he seems to smile. He has a quick and piercing eye."

PART TWO

REBEL

CHAPTER FIVE

SHIVAJI was now nineteen. He seems never to have wavered in his ambitions, in his resolute confidence in himself. But he told no one of his plans. Dadaji saw in him a promising youth who could be sure of a fine career in the service of the Mussulman Government. He would be a noted soldier like his father and grandfather, rising, in spite of his religion, to the highest posts of command, respected and admired by all his fellow Hindus. Jijabai and Shivaji may have talked together of their dream of Hindu freedom—an independent Hindu State, but to any man of the world this would have seemed fantastic—a delightful dream, no doubt, but an obvious impossibility. For consider the odds. With the exception of a few chieftains in the far south, there were no Hindu states. The Rajputs had long since submitted to the sword of Islam, and their princes were glad of a post in the Imperial forces and flattered when their daughters were demanded for the Imperial harem. In the Maratha country there was apparently little desire for change. People were resigned to the present; it was too long since there had been a Hindu king for any one to appreciate the distinction of independence; the façade of the Muslim courts, whether of Delhi or of Bijapur, impressed people with a sense of prosperity, stability and vast resources. A force of Maratha peasants and half-armed hillmen would hardly be a match even for the local governor with his Abyssinian mercenaries. . . .

Shivaji's estate was in an enclave of the frontier, surrounded by forts which were garrisoned by Bijapur troops. These forts served not only to guard the frontier, but also to overawe the local population. To the west of Poona was a cluster of forts in the mountain range of the Sahyadris, the range dividing the plateau of Central India from the strip of low-lying coastland. It was obviously important for any government whose territories extended over both plateau and coastland to hold in strength the mountain bridge between them. Shivaji was already, in his quiet, purposeful manner, preparing his first moves against the Mussulman Government. He saw that a rebel's only chance, even of temporary success, was to gain a foothold in that mountain bridge.

To the south-west of Poona was a small fort called Torna—rough walls of great uncut stones and a barracks on a flat-topped hill, commanding one of the mountain passes. Cool in the summer, it was an uncomfortable place when the rains broke. Then the winding hill-paths became impassable; no traders came from the hill villages to sell vegetables or fresh meat to the garrison; and, crouching in their bare, rain-swept quarters, the soldiers clustered round braziers, drew their cloaks tighter round them and grumbled and cursed. The commander was as dissatisfied as his men. There was no war nor any apparent disaffection among the local population. It was tedious waiting through the long months of the monsoon with no occupation and no change of company. Finally, in the rains of 1646, the commander's patience gave out. Without reporting his action to headquarters, he marched his troops down to the plains, intending to return to Torna Fort as soon as the monsoon waned. With a band of hillmen whom he had been secretly training for some time, Shivaji slipped into the abandoned fort and seized the arsenal and treasury. Now he could reward his followers with arms and money.

The Mussulman commander, as soon as he was notified of this extraordinary action, reported Shivaji to Bijapur. Even Shivaji's tutor, Dadaji, was taken by surprise, and sent a message of astonished reproof to his pupil. Receiving no reply, Dadaji wrote excitedly to Shivaji's father, warning him of the trouble ahead. Shahaji paid little attention to this letter. His son had always been troublesome; now he had got into a scrape, and it was for the authorities to deal with him.

Meanwhile Shivaji sent a messenger to Bijapur

to justify his conduct. He protested his loyalty, and explained that he had merely entered the fort as a demonstration against the incapacity of the commander. A soldier who left his post just because he found the weather trying was hardly to be entrusted with any responsible office. It is not necessary to discuss whether Shivaji hoped to deceive any one with these ingenuous excuses. His object was to gain time. The Bijapur authorities were sufficiently irritated with their commander to listen while Shivaji's agent multiplied accusations and recriminations against that wretched officer. Moreover, with funds drawn from the captured treasury, various officials of the Durbar were bribed to prolong the inquiry. Charges and countercharges were exchanged, while Shivaji worked feverishly all that monsoon fortifying a hill called Rajgad, six miles from Torna and guarding the approach to it from the direction of Bijapur.

Eleven miles south-west of Poona was the next great Mussulman fortress, Kondana or Sinhgad, famous in Indian history, the Lion-Fort. Shivaji bribed its Muhammadan governor to admit him, and took possession of the fortress without even a scuffle.

The last frontier fortress south of Poona was Purandar. The governor, a hard and cruel man who had caused his wife to be blown from a gun for some trivial offence, had recently died. The office was hereditary, and his three sons were now involved in a violent quarrel over the succession to their father's post. Each had sent agents to Bijapur to represent his own claims; but in the dilatory manner of a Mussulman durbar, no immediate reply was given, clerks busily wrote out petitions and counter-petitions, precedents were quoted and discussed, and bribes went briskly round. The three sons were left in exasperating uncertainty, none anxious to leave the fort and so seem to surrender his claim, yet tormented by the strain of living together, suspicious and hostile. Their quarrels became increasingly violent. With agreeable effrontery, Shivaji offered his services as arbitrator. Such an offer would ordinarily, one imagines, have been answered with the snub its impertinence deserved. But, exhausted with the tension, the three brothers seem to have welcomed any way of ending an intolerable situation. Shivaji was invited to the fort as a guest during the merrymaking of the Feast of Lamps. This festival occurs after the end of the monsoon. Shivaji accepted. As a shield against the monsoon storms, it was usual, then as now, to protect all buildings against rain with thatch. Bands of coolies, carrying on their heads grass for the thatching, climbed up the hill paths and were admitted into the fortress. For some weeks past some of Shivaji's followers had been unobtrusively mingling with the coolies, stripped naked to the waist like them, bending under great bundles of grass. But in these bundles they had concealed their weapons. The sentries were not accustomed to examine each coolie; and now they had no reason for suspicion.

Meanwhile the two younger brothers were meditating treachery against the eldest, who, they feared, would inevitably be chosen by any fair arbitrator to succeed their father. A banquet was given to welcome Shivaji as their guest. At this festival the usually sober Marathas were accustomed to drink deeply. A virtuous English captain[1] was once shocked at their potations. (Can they really have been greater than those of the captain's own English troopers?) "They revel," he wrote severely, "through the night in a state of low debauchery, which would hardly be envied by the keenest votaries of *Comus* and his beastly crew." During such a "revel" the younger brothers picked a quarrel with the eldest brother, fell upon him and tied him with ropes. Then they turned to Shivaji and prepared to bargain with him. It is unlikely that Shivaji had been drinking much; his ascetic diet was remarked on by all who met him. He met the drunken and excited offers of the two brothers with feigned surprise. He suggested that any immediate decision was unnecessary—as arbitrator he had to consider his award—and he invited the two brothers

[1] See Broughton, *Letters from a Maratha Camp.*

to a bathing party next day. They bathed in a stream which ran by the walls of the fortress. The water ran cool and cloudy after the monsoon rain, the banks were gay with wild begonia, and over the hillside the bracken was a wave of emerald. Shivaji and the brothers bathed together as if nothing had happened the night before, and, talking and laughing happily, they climbed back towards the fortress gates. The two brothers stopped and stared. The Bijapur flag with its Ottoman crescent had disappeared from the gate towers. There were strange soldiers on guard, wild-looking hillmen. But whose soldiers? Shivaji explained blandly that they were his. When the brothers burst into angry expostulation at the trick, Shivaji reminded them of their conduct to their eldest brother. Then, with his usual amused contempt for those he outwitted, he offered all three brothers small estates elsewhere, with which they seem to have been satisfied. The regular garrison of the fort, outnumbered by Shivaji's men and having, one can assume, little enthusiasm for the leadership of the disorderly brothers, enlisted eagerly under Shivaji's banner. They were mercenaries, and this young Maratha adventurer must have seemed an attractive leader.

So within a year, while the Bijapur authorities debated the rights and wrongs of Shivaji's seizure of Torna, Shivaji had, without bloodshed, made himself master of the bridge of strong forts connecting the eastern plateau with the coastland and guarding the approaches from Bijapur to Shivaji's own lands.

The lethargy of the government may seem strange, but we must shed all modern preconceptions of efficiency and means of accurate information. It should be remembered how even in the eighteenth century battles were fought between the forces of rival western states before war was declared, or in ignorance that peace had been signed. The organisation of the Bijapur kingdom was very loose, the military establishment depending partly on mercenaries and partly on the levies of territorial magnates. Where a fort, for instance, was held by a local magnate, it was of little urgency to the government who that magnate was so long as he professed loyalty and sent regularly the taxes collected from that locality. Shivaji kept up a running stream of excuses for his actions, and not only made a great show of his loyalty, but promised to send more taxes than his predecessors in the various forts had ever collected. At the worst no one imagined that Shivaji had any purpose except the prosecution of some dispute with the local officials. He had moved very quickly and without any apparent violence, so that the whole position was still obscure. Moreover, every one in the capital was far less interested in the escapades of a petty landowner near the frontier than in a mysterious illness which had attacked the Sultan of Bijapur. It is said that his life was only saved by the arts of a devoted sorcerer named Hashim Uluvi, who magically transferred some of the years of his own life to that of his prince. . . .

Some time in the following year (1647) Shivaji's tutor, Dadaji, fell ill. He was a very old man now, and the anxieties of recent months had enfeebled him. Shivaji nursed him with the devotion of a son. Turning his pale eyes on Shivaji, the old man said faintly that if he had spoken harshly to him about the seizure of the Bijapur forts it had been in Shivaji's interest; and while Shivaji stammered out a request for forgiveness if he had caused his tutor any anxiety, the prescience of the dying inspired Dadaji to a sudden realisation of Shivaji's destiny, and he adjured him, when he rose in the end to great power, to restore the old virtues of Hindu life. Then he blessed him and died.

Shivaji felt the loss of Dadaji very keenly. He knew how much he owed to him. The outer courtyard of the palace at Poona must have seemed sadly changed now that there were no longer rolls of Sanskrit verse piled against the wall, no longer the low desk where Dadaji sat for so many hours working at accounts, puzzling over reports from various districts of the estate. Of course, there was always in the inner courtyard his mother; and, indeed, his wife, for Shivaji had married (we do not know when or where) a girl called Saibai, a gentle, selfless creature who seems to have lived quietly and unobtrusively in Jijabai's shadow. The Marathas have never tolerated purdah, and many of their women have taken dramatic parts in history; but a wife of a retiring nature, who has no ambitions outside her house, cannot afford much material for the historian, and Maratha annalists have passed over Saibai with a few words of conventional commendation. Of her, as of so many queens in Indian history, might be quoted the epitaph so little appropriate to its author that the Empress Nur Jahan composed for her own mausoleum: "On the grave of that poor little one there will be neither the voice of a nightingale nor the wings of a moth."

CHAPTER SIX

SHIVAJI'S first successes had exhilarated the Hindus of the neighbouring districts, and many young Marathas left their ploughs and young Brahmans their books to enlist under him. His difficulty was how to pay and provide rations for his increasing following. From his fortress bridge he began to look east over the rich low-lying strip of coastland.

This territory had been less ravaged in the late war, and now its wealth formed a great contrast to the upland plateau. Along the coast were forts and emporia; caravans from Africa and Arabia wound along the red-soiled roads under heavy banyan trees whose grey spidery roots hung aquiver in the wind, their red berries pattering whenever a flight of parrots landed noisily on the gunmetal-coloured bark; Persian and Abyssinian merchants lived at ease in great houses, the outer walls gay with painted flowers and trees. The capital of this province was Kalyan, a town known long before to the Greeks as a trading centre for brass, blackwood and fine brocade. It had now entered on a period of gentle decline. The younger Muhammadans left it to seek their fortunes at court in Bijapur; and in the streets there was only the lazy movement of provincial life. In a climate with little change, winter or summer, warm and damp and enervating, the gardens were famous for their rich flowers and enormous trees. A slow river moved between sleek-shining mudbanks lined with palms, and the thatched cottages of fishermen raised on stakes. Dhows from Zanzibar and Muscat rode at anchor, while high-prowed fishing-boats moved downstream, the noise of their oars distinct in the drowsy noon. Over the crumbling city walls a few banners, stamped with the crescent device of Bijapur, stirred in the sea-wind.

On a warm afternoon of 1648 the governor of the province, Mulana Ahmed, an Arab in the service of the Sultan, dozed in his palace. He had, a few days ago, superintended the dispatch of a special caravan to Bijapur, carrying the year's revenue of his province. This was (as far as the central authorities were concerned) his chief duty, and as usual he had sent a strong guard in attendance. The caravan moved towards a pass in the hills leading to the plateau beyond and thence to Bijapur. From the flat coastland the hills towered up, gaunt basalt rocks leaping from a tangle of forest, and round the highest peaks a faint coronet of clouds. A wild stretch of country, one would not venture there alone, but in that well-armed company there can have been no thought of an alarm. As they entered the pass the guards thought of little but the labour of the ascent and the heat of the day. They did not notice any movement at the mouth of the pass behind them.

But Shivaji, with three hundred men mounted on little Maratha ponies, was stalking them up the narrowing ravine. The creak and rumble of cart wheels, steady tramp of feet, crackling of dried leaves and scurry of wild things into farther thickets, and then suddenly a roar from the rear, the battlecry that was one day to be feared all over India: "Hurr! Hurr! Mahadev!" and the Marathas were upon the startled soldiers. The fight was soon over, and the caravan with its great treasure in Shivaji's hands. He lost ten men killed in this, his first battle. He gave generous rewards of money to his followers and presented large sums to the families of the ten who had fallen.

Meanwhile, in the town of Kalyan, the bazaars were empty in the heat of noon. A party of Maratha horsemen rode quietly in at the gates, secured the sentries in the guard-rooms on the walls, and rode on to the palace and took the governor prisoner. When the merchants stirred from their houses in the cool of the evening they found a young Maratha called Abaji installed in the palace and an ochre flag fluttering over the city gates.

A day or two later Shivaji himself arrived in Kalyan. The Arab governor's daughter-in-law was still in the palace. She was brought before Shivaji.

She was famous for her great beauty. Shivaji rose at her entrance. Smiling, he said, "Ah, if only my mother had been half as beautiful as you, I should not be the ugly little fellow that I am." Then he ordered that ceremonial presents should be given to her, and had her sent with a guard of honour to her relatives. To the dispossessed governor Shivaji behaved with equal chivalry. He released him and sent him with an escort to Bijapur.

The attack on the revenue caravan and the capture of Kalyan were acts of open rebellion which Shivaji did not attempt to explain away as he had his previous conduct.

The deposed Governor of Kalyan, Mulana Ahmed, made a dramatic appearance in the Sultan's Durbar clad in mourning. He advanced to the foot of the throne, cast his turban before him and, striking his mouth repeatedly with the palm of his hand, clamoured for vengeance on the rebel who had so easily and almost casually dispossessed him. The Sultan at once sent a messenger ordering Shivaji to present himself at Court. Then, as he awaited Shivaji's reply, the Sultan remembered that Shivaji's own father was actually in Bijapur service. He caused him to be arrested and brought before the Durbar. Shahaji, sincerely enough, protested his innocence of any knowledge of Shivaji's misdeeds. Indeed he must have been as horrified as any other noble at court to hear of his son's outrageous behaviour. But he begged the Sultan not to attribute to him any share of blame. He reminded him how he had sent Shivaji away from Bijapur because he had been so unruly a child. Since then he had not seen him. He had given him a good tutor; it was impossible to understand; the boy must have gone crazy. He even urged the Sultan to send at once a strong force to capture Shivaji. This obviously sensible advice was too straightforward for the Sultan. He became more suspicious. A father must be aware of his son's doings, he argued. And the Mussulman nobles round his throne, especially the foreign adventurers, the Turks and Afghans and Abyssinians, resentful and jealous of the high office held by a local man, a Hindu, warned the Sultan of treachery. Still protesting his innocence, Shahaji was dragged from the Durbar hall and put in irons.

It is clear that at this stage the Bijapur authorities had only to act with vigour and there could have been an end of Shivaji and his band of hillmen. Whatever Shivaji's gifts, his followers were as yet no match for regular soldiers; they were untrained, undisciplined, ill-armed and accustomed to Muhammadan victory and domination. A few forts taken and a caravan looted had given them a little confidence, but that would have soon ebbed at the sight of Turkish artillery. But no one in Bijapur believed that there was any serious trouble brewing.

In the tortuous story of Shivaji's rise to power one must always remember how differently men three centuries ago regarded loyalty to the state from their descendants of to-day. Shivaji's contemporaries, Condé and Turenne, could fight sometimes for their own country and sometimes for Spain—their loyalty or disloyalty was generally a matter either of hard bargaining or of political manœuvre. Similar relations between the official class and the central authority continued in Turkey on into the nineteenth century. Readers of Mr. William Plomer's admirable *Ali the Lion* will remember how Ali disposed of various Ottoman officials and, far from being regarded as a rebel, was generally confirmed in the posts of the men he had expelled. So, in the Bijapur kingdom, however angry the Sultan might be at the *manner* of Shivaji's outbreak, no one regarded Shivaji yet as a declared enemy of the state—at worst a troublesome young fool who had taken up banditry.[1] There was, in the opinion of the Sultan's advisers, no need at all for military action; and they hit upon a clever and inexpensive way of dealing with Shivaji. Shahaji was taken from his prison and told that he would be bricked up alive unless Shivaji presented himself in Bijapur.

[1] It is also necessary to remember that melodramatic *gestures* against public security move Eastern sensibility even to-day less than Western. For instance, an Indian peasant whose wife has deserted him will put a pebble on a railway line, hoping to derail a train just to show his opinion of life. And Indian juries are far less disapproving of such a gesture than English judges.

Again he protested his innocence and was told: "Write a letter summoning your son. Explain to him your predicament. Unless he comes here you will die." So Shahaji wrote in a naturally alarmed strain to Shivaji, and he was then carried into a niche in the wall in which he could just stand. He was chained to the back of the niche, and masons began to brick up the entrance. For intervals of several days the masons broke off their work while the authorities waited for Shivaji's arrival. There was no sign of him yet; so the masons returned to add a new layer of bricks. At last there was only room for one more brick, and that last brick would shut out light and air for ever from the prisoner. It is easy to imagine Shivaji's anxiety and indecision. If he surrendered himself he would probably be executed—not so much as punishment for any misdeeds, but, in the manner of an Oriental court, as a precaution against future trouble. On the other hand, the Sultan would certainly carry out his threat and have Shahaji buried alive; and the thought of his father's eyes, glimpsed dimly in the shadows of that last dark slot between the bricks, moving feverishly in anguish and suspense, must have moved him deeply, for all that he owed him little duty or affection. After all, even if he had been little of a father to him, it was only because he was his father that he was now awaiting death by slow suffocation. At first he seems to have decided that there was no alternative; he must go to Bijapur, even if it meant dying in his father's stead. It is said that it was only the wild entreaties of his wife Saibai that made him hesitate; and there was also the calculating Jijabai—she had little cause to love her husband and a great love for Shivaji. She reminded him of his dreams and ambitions—it was not only his life that was at stake—it was Hindu independence.

While Shivaji hesitated a sudden inspiration came to him.

He sent a messenger galloping northward to the Court of the Great Mogul. He begged to be allowed to tender his submission to the Emperor and become his subject. In token of his devotion to the Imperial cause he offered to hand over the frontier fortresses on the Bijapur side of the frontier to Imperial officers.

It will be remembered that in the last war the Emperor Shah Jehan had failed to reduce Bijapur to complete dependence and had rested contented with a formal submission. But one day there might be another dispute: the tribute might be withheld—the Bijapur Sultan might renew pretensions to independence when the attention of the Imperial Government was engaged, say on the north-west frontier. A few fortresses in the difficult hill-country on the road to Bijapur would be invaluable.

Shivaji's messenger was treated with flattering consideration at the Imperial Court. The Emperor's son, Prince Murad Baksh, Viceroy of Central India, wrote gracious letters not only to Shivaji, but also, further to embarrass Bijapur, to Shivaji's father imprisoned in the brick wall. It was a strange reversal of fortune for Shahaji. An Imperial letter could not be withheld. The stiff sheet, bordered with elegant designs and stamped with a great purple hand arrogantly outspread, had to be treated with the same respect as an utterance of the Emperor from his throne, the lofty balcony—the throne known as "The Seat of the Shadow of God," from which the Emperor addressed India. In the letter to Shahaji Prince Murad wrote: "Be free from anxiety. A dress of honour has been sent to you as a mark of Our favour. We trust that by its good-omened arrival you will appreciate the extent of Our Imperial condescension." And to Shivaji: "You, Shivaji, worthy of magnanimous treatment, recipient of Our favour, have implored Imperial help, and your letter is pleasing to Us. . . ."[1]

It was far from pleasing to the Bijapur authorities. They were greatly alarmed at this sudden Mogul interest in the internal affairs of Bijapur. If Shivaji really handed over the frontier forts at present in his possession, Mogul troops of the border garrisons could enter and fortify them before any effective Bijapur forces could arrive.

But worse than the cordial letter, worse even than

[1] Kincaid and Parasnis.

the robe of honour, was the fact that the Emperor had conferred on Shahaji a post at the Court in Delhi. This meant that Shahaji would now be claimed as a citizen of the Empire and the Bijapur Government held responsible for his safety. The Sultan of Bijapur had no alternative but to order Shahaji's release from his tomb of brick.

The position was now curious. If Shivaji carried out his proposed transfer of allegiance to the Emperor his father's life and safety would lose all value as a bargaining point, and Shahaji would almost certainly be re-arrested and killed. On the other hand, the Emperor might presently demand the performance of Shivaji's promises; and, while real submission to the Empire would be a serious reverse for Shivaji's policy, active resistance to an Imperial army was not yet practicable. So Shivaji in the following months had to pursue a course of extraordinary difficulty. He sent flattering and obsequious letters to Delhi as though to distract the attention of the Emperor from the fact that in spite of his frequently-expressed devotion to Imperial interests those border fortresses remained still in his own hands. Nor did he take any hostile action against Bijapur; and, for their part, the Bijapur authorities, whatever their opinion of the success of Shivaji's manœuvre, were careful not to move against Shivaji for fear of him carrying out his threat of submitting to the Moguls.

CHAPTER SEVEN

DURING the year 1649, while this distrustful pause continued between Shivaji and his Mussulman neighbours, Shivaji met two men whose fame in Western India is almost as great as Shivaji's own. These were the poet Tukaram and the Saint Ramdas.

The local cults of the Maratha country had been inseparably connected both with the birth of a Marathi literature and the gradually awakening national consciousness. These cults centred round Pandharpur, where Krishna was worshipped. A succession of saints and poets, living and teaching there, had made the place holy. Chokhamela, a man of the lowest caste, taught the unity of all mankind and is supposed to have been welcomed into the temple of Krishna by a miraculous gesture of the image. Dnyandev's commentaries have become the foundation of the ideals and morality of modern Hinduism.

An interesting figure in the rise of Marathi literature was the Jesuit, Father Stevens, the first Englishman known to have visited India, and the only Englishman to write a considerable poem in any Indian language.[1] In 1615, twelve years before Shivaji's birth, Father Stevens had published a

[1] Steven's life is related in the introduction to Saldanha's *Christian Purana*.

dialect-Marathi edition of the *Harrowing of Hell*, which, in spite of the change of climate and atmosphere inevitable in an Oriental version, still retains much of the heavy grandeur of the old nordic legends from which Stevens took his theme. A Catholic, Stevens had left England to escape the Elizabethan proscriptions. He studied at Douai, and worked in Rome under Campion before joining the Jesuit Mission in the Indies. For all his studies in European culture and his Latin training, he surrendered to the charm of the freshly-developing Marathi language. "Like a jewel among pebbles," he wrote, "like a sapphire among jewels, is the excellence of the Marathi tongue. Like the jasmine among blossoms, the musk among perfumes, the peacock among birds, the Zodiac among the stars, is Marathi among languages."

If Marathi so impressed a foreigner with its beauty, it is not difficult to imagine the exhilaration with which Marathas hailed the new literature that was springing up, a literature expressed in their natural tongue and no longer buried in the learned profundities of Sanskrit, a literature that found utterance for the new consciousness of race and religion.

Tukaram,[1] whose poems are still sung in every Maratha village, was the son of a grocer. As a

[1] These sketches of Tukaram and Randas are based on the account in Kincaid and Parasnis.

child he sauntered dreamily about the countryside, his thoughts turning incessantly to a life of religion. When he was still young his father died and he was left with the family shop to manage. He had neither taste nor ability for business. Many families in the village had accounts with the shop, but Tukaram was too shy ever to approach any one for settlement of a debt. Whenever he had any money he gave it away in charity. The last small sum that remained between him and destitution he gave to rescue a priest from the debtor's prison. Then, penniless and starving, he took a pilgrim's staff and wandered away into the hills, composing as he went the songs that have made him famous. Villagers and poor herdsmen, with the ready charity of the East, provided him with sustenance, sat round listening to his verses and returned to spread his fame. One day a minstrel recited one of Tukaram's poems to Shivaji, who was so moved by it that he sent a messenger begging Tukaram to come and make his home with him, promising him wealth and comfort. Tukaram replied with a poem:

"Prince, your torches, umbrellas of state and richly-caparisoned horses, your pomp and splendour and kingly ways are not for me. I have fled from the world, and you would entice me back. Ah, let me be alone, solitary, in silence. You promise me robes of state and a palace. These would be wasted on me. Forests and meadows are my dwellings.

Moss-grown rocks are my couch. The sky above me is my cloak."

When Shivaji read this he remained for a while in silence. Then he left his camp and wandered alone over the rolling yellow downland of the Maratha plateau till he found Tukaram. He fell at his feet. He tore his clothes and put on the rags of an ascetic and sat humbly and in silence beside the poet. Neither spoke. And here Shivaji's followers found their master after a long and anxious search. They begged him to return to his camp. He would not listen to them. In despair they sent word to Shivaji's mother, beseeching her to add her entreaties to theirs. Jijabai came and upbraided her son. He had encouraged his followers to rebel against the Muhammadan and now he was abandoning them; there were many saints in Hindu India, but only one man with the destiny of Shivaji; the Hindu cause now needed heroes and armies rather than minstrels and hermits. Sorrowfully Shivaji acknowledged the justice of her arguments and returned with his followers. He did not again see Tukaram, who died that same year. But for the rest of his life he remained in close contact with Ramdas, Tukaram's saintly contemporary whom he also met in 1649.

Ramdas, even as a child, showed his inclination for the life of an ascetic. He fled from home to avoid an early marriage, and spent his youth visiting on foot the various shrines of India. He finally settled down in a temple of the Hero-God Rama, near Satara. He is said to have worked miracles even as a child, and his temple-home became a centre of pilgrimage. As soon as he heard of him, Shivaji wrote to Ramdas, who replied, as Tukaram had done, with a poem. But, while Tukaram sang the praises of obscurity Ramdas acclaimed, as though with a flourish of trumpets, the new hero-king who would free the Hindus. With the poem he sent a present of a handful of earth, of pebbles and of horse-dung. Shivaji was sitting with his mother when this unusual gift arrived. Jijabai, for all her religious enthusiasm, was a literal-minded woman. Indignantly she stared at Ramdas' present and asked if this was a proper thing to send to a gentleman. But Shivaji, after a moment's thought, said, "It is a symbol and a prophecy. The earth means that I shall conquer all this land. The pebbles are the fortresses with which I shall hold it, and the horse-dung signifies my cavalry for which I shall become famous."

Shivaji wrote constantly to Ramdas, asking his advice on matters of government, administration and policy. At the height of his power he visited Ramdas and, bowing before him, gave him a document which was a deed bestowing on the saint all his kingdom. Ramdas said, "I accept the gift on behalf of God. Take back your kingdom and rule in His name. Govern, not as an unfettered autocrat, but humbly as the deputy of Heaven."

To mark his reverence for Ramdas' cult, Shivaji made all his followers greet each other with the word "Ram," and to this day all Marathas, in their salutations, continue to obey Shivaji's direction. Modern Totalitarians would perhaps express surprise that the Marathas should choose for their word of greeting not the name of a successful ruler, but that of a saint. Finally, in tribute to the pilgrims who thronged round Ramdas, Shivaji chose as the national banner of his kingdom the ochre flag that Hindu pilgrims bear on their long wanderings, and this plain yellow flag became regarded by Marathas with something of the mystic awe of contemporary France for the oriflamme.

In spite of the character of a crusade which Ramdas's blessings gave to Shivaji's long struggle, it is remarkable how little religious animosity or intolerance Shivaji displayed. His kindness to Catholic priests is an agreeable contrast to the proscriptions of the Hindu priesthood in the (largely Marathi-speaking) Indian territories of the Portuguese. Even his enemies remarked on his extreme respect for Mussulman priests, for mosques and for the Koran. The Muslim historian Khafi Khan, who cannot mention Shivaji in his chronicle without adding epithets of vulgar abuse, nevertheless acknowledges that Shivaji never entered a conquered town without taking measures to safeguard the mosques from damage; whenever a Koran came into his possession he treated it with the same respect as if it had been one of the sacred works of his own faith; and that whenever his men captured Mussulman ladies they were brought to Shivaji, who looked after them as if they were his wards till he could return them to their relations. It is perhaps worth remembering that this century in Europe was noteworthy for the activities of Tilly in Germany and of Cromwell in Ireland.

CHAPTER EIGHT

IN 1650 Prince Aurangzeb, destined to be the last of the Moguls, to crush the southern principalities of Golconda and Bijapur, and to drag down his Empire in ruins in his efforts to quell the Marathas, succeeded his brother Murad as Viceroy of Central India.

Aurangzeb had many of the gifts of his great dynasty. He was able, industrious, and of Spartan endurance. But his great qualities were overshadowed by his devotion to an archaic bitter creed. All the cultural development of Islam, all its philosophy and gaiety and grandeur of soul, meant nothing to him. His religion was that of a nomad chieftain, an Arab guerrilero. He hated, with a Puritan's personal and intense passion, all music and art and beauty. He averted his eyes with a shudder from everything that might remind him of the refrain of the poets of Islam that the Creator Himself must be a poet. As he grew older his asceticism became almost inhuman. Pledging himself to restore on earth the apostolic poverty of Omar, he took nothing for his needs from the huge treasury of the Empire, but to earn himself a little pocket-money he knitted caps which he sold to his nobles. He slept on the naked earth, covered only with a tiger-skin. On his accession to the Peacock Throne his first decree was against the use of wine which his predecessors had not only permitted to be sold openly, but had often, in spite of the Prophet's ban, themselves enjoyed. Aurangzeb, reproving his people in the manner of an ancient Hebrew prophet for their wine-bibbing, added: "This evil practice is so common, that there are only two men in India who are not drunkards—myself and the Chief Justice."

He had, however, overestimated the number of righteous men in his Empire. "With respect to the Chief Justice," noted that agreeable gossip, Manucci, "the Emperor was in error, for I myself sent him every day a bottle of spirits which he drank in secret." Even his favourite wife, the Georgian Princess Udepuri, was a confirmed drunkard, and sometimes Aurangzeb found her "all in disorder, her hair flying loose and her head full of drink." With a gentleness rare in him he would sit by her couch, his hand on her forehead; but she was too far gone in drunkenness to distinguish between her husband and her servants, and would reply to his reproving endearments with cries for more wine.

The second decree regulated the length of beards. No Mussulman, ran the *firman*, should wear a beard longer than four finger-breadths; and the police stood about in the streets with measuring instruments and shears. Many of the nobles who were proud of their luxuriant beards had to simulate colds and hide their beards under shawls which they pretended were necessary to protect their throats.

A third decree prohibited music of all kinds, and ordered the destructions of all musical instruments. A crowd gathered round the palace, lamenting. Aurangzeb asked the reason for the demonstration and was told: "We are mourning for the death of poor Lady Music." Unsmiling, Aurangzeb replied, "Let her be well and truly buried."[1]

These decrees were, however, still in the future, and no one could yet have guessed that Aurangzeb would ever reach the Peacock Throne, for he was the third of the Imperial Princes. But they are worth relating here as most characteristic of the man. From the moment of his appointment as Viceroy he represented, as far as the south of India was concerned, Imperial foreign policy; for his vigour and determination were in striking contrast to the increasing lethargy of the dilettante Emperor.

The court of the Viceroy was transformed. Aurangzeb himself rose and bathed before dawn, prayed and then took a light meal. He was a vegetarian, and never ate at any meal more than a few herbs and green vegetables. Then for two hours he sat with his secretaries. At midday he prayed again, and then dined. All afternoon he transacted business

[1] Manucci.

in his audience chamber till the evening prayer. He was never so happy as at his devotions. He prayed in "a private faire room, upon goodly Jet stone, having onely a Persian Lamb-skinne under him. . . . He turneth over his Beads and saith three thousand two hundred words, according to the number of his Beads." He seldom slept more than two hours, and spent most of the night reading the Koran. He never wore spectacles till he was over eighty, and the favourite pose in which contemporary painters depicted him was bowed over some religious work, the long neck curved, the thin, bony face thrust forward, the dark, heavy-lidded eyes peering. Endless work, prayer, religious exercises—an almost superhuman physical endurance. No wonder several of the palace eunuchs told the Neapolitan visitor, Dr. Careri, "*Qu'ils croient que leur Maitre, qui avait la reputation d'être habile dans la Necromancie, étoit aidé du Démon, pour soutenir une vie si impossible.*"

His face never betrayed any emotion. All the time in public he would sit with shoulders hunched up, his chin on his chest, eyelids drooping. If any one addressed him he would think over his answers in silence, and then suddenly jerk up his head and straighten his back. And whatever he said then, wrote Manucci, left no opening for a reply.

He was curiously proud of his power of dissimulation, which to most people seems hardly a quality worthy of an Emperor. Himself he wrote,

"One cannot rule without deception. A government depending on cunning will last for ever."

Sincerely and devotedly religious, he killed his brothers and imprisoned his father without a qualm, for, believing himself the instrument of the Almighty, he was as convinced of his own virtue as Robespierre; and no incidental violence should deflect him from his manifest mission, to chastise the heathen and re-establish the Faith in its original simplicity. Like Philip II. in the Escorial, indefatigable and obtuse, he grappled with the problems of an Empire from the single viewpoint of religion. As he lay dying the full sincerity, and also the pathos, of his lonely Puritanism is most evident. "I know not who I am," he wrote to his son, "where I shall go or what will happen to me, a sinner full of sins. . . . My years have gone by profitless. God has been in my heart, yet my darkened eyes have not recognised His light. I have greatly sinned, and know not what torment awaits me." [1]

From the moment of Aurangzeb's appointment as Viceroy there was a sinister activity in the fortresses and blockhouses on the Mogul side of the border. Shivaji may be excused for alarm at this evidence of warlike preparation, for his relations with the Mogul authorities were equivocal. He wrote to

[1] This impression of Aurangzeb is drawn from the accounts of Bernier and Manucci, from the *Voyage autour du Monde*, by Dr. Gemelli-Careri, and from the Emperor's own letters (Ed. J. Billimoria).

Aurangzeb, once more protesting his attachment to the Imperial cause, and reminding the new Viceroy how gracious his predecessor had been to him and his father. Aurangzeb replied vaguely but formally. He was not interested in a petty Hindu landowner, whose only force appeared to be a band of hill-men. His eyes were turned farther south, towards Bijapur.

The dynasty of Bijapur (in spite of their Ottoman descent, regardless of the proud position of the Caliph with whom they claimed relationship as defender of the orthodox faith) had embraced Shi'ism, and so were hated as heretics by the Puritan northerners. To Aurangzeb their heresy was but one item in the indictment against them. Utterly hateful to him was their city with its public baths and Byzantine refinements, its idolatrous ceremonies and frescoes painted by foreign infidels depicting heathen gods reclining in flowering meadows and Greek goddesses with white naked limbs. He thought of the Court of Bijapur in much the same way as in contemporary England various Sergeant Obadiahs regarded the court of Charles II.

It must have been early obvious to the Bijapur Government that with the arrival of Aurangzeb a second war with the Moguls was inevitable. Obviously the first thing, then, to be done was to settle the question of Shivaji, whether one admitted the position of semi-independence he had taken up or not; for the territories of which he was in virtual control lay along the route of Mogul invasion. Instead of either conciliating or crushing Shivaji, a feeble attempt was made to have Shivaji assassinated. A Maratha was bribed to waylay him, but the attempt failed.

Now, as it happened, this would-be assassin had passed through the territories of a Hindu hill chief called More. When Shivaji was a child his mother had suggested a marriage between him and one of More's daughters. More refused, and relations between the two families became strained. Whether jealous of the sudden rise of a man whom he had rejected for a son-in-law, or whether bribed by Bijapur, More certainly allowed the preparations for Shivaji's assassination to be made in his fief.

Shivaji used this pretext to present More with an ultimatum, requiring him to enter into immediate alliance with him. There were prolonged negotiations, and it is clear that neither party was sincere after one had just connived at the attempted murder of the other. But Shivaji wanted to force More's hand. After some time his spies told him what he wanted to know—that More had appealed to Bijapur for help against Shivaji. Now he could claim that More had initiated hostilities, and, marching into the More fief, he surrounded the chief town of it with his troops.

His envoys were still haggling with More; but when Shivaji's sudden advance was reported, More broke out into querulous complaints. They had been drinking, and tempers were strained. The envoys replied with accusations of treachery and communication with Bijapur. Finally one of the envoys drew his sword and killed More, and in the ensuing confusion the envoys escaped. Shortly afterwards Shivaji entered the town and received its submission.

Historians hostile to Shivaji have seized on this incident to accuse Shivaji of premeditated assassination. There is no proof of this. Shivaji certainly intended to annex More's dominions, and he could have done this without resorting to an unnecessary act of treachery; and few men were less vindictive than Shivaji. Probably the best refutation of this charge is to be found in the subsequent attitude of More's steward, Baji Prabhu. This man, noted for his integrity, surrendered to Shivaji, and became his devoted adherent, finally laying down his life for him in the defile of Rangana, which Marathas speak of as Greeks did of Thermopylæ. It is unlikely that a man of Baji's qualities would have served so loyally a man guilty of planning the murder of his former master. Even, however, if Shivaji did plan More's murder, it must be remembered that contemporary opinion would have condoned this as a proper retaliation for More's privity to the attempt on Shivaji.

The whole affair which had begun with Bijapur

effort to dispose of Shivaji ended with Shivaji's strength considerably increased and the possibility of compromise or conciliation very remote.

In 1656 Prince Aurangzeb was ready for an attack on Bijapur. Fortune provided him with a pretext. In November of that year the Sultan died and was succeeded by a boy of nineteen, the pathetic Ali. His accession was attended by widespread disorder and by faction fights in the city itself. Aurangzeb wrote to his father, pointing out that Bijapur was a tributary state of the Empire, and that the new king had mounted his throne without the permission of the Emperor and without renewing his father's act of submission. He added that the Prince was illegitimate (which was almost certainly untrue), and that in the general confusion of the kingdom its conquest would only be a military promenade. Shah Jehan agreed, and in February, 1657, the Mogul forces crossed the border.

A Mogul army of that period differed little in composition and organisation from European armies of thirty or forty years before. The chief military strength of the Empire lay in artillery. It was with Turkish guns and gunners that Babar had conquered India and founded the Mogul dynasty. But by the seventeenth century many of the gunners were European. Dr. Careri, who visited Aurangzeb's camp, found English, French, German, Dutch and

Portuguese gunners there. Some had come in search of fortune and adventure; others were deserted sailors or escaped convicts from Goa. They were by contemporary standards very highly paid, each "Frankish" gunner receiving two hundred rupees a month.[1] It was seldom that Indian officers were entrusted with the command of batteries, and even when they were, their pay was much less than that of their European fellow-officers. In the Grand Army of the Empire there were sixty to seventy pieces of light artillery and three hundred of heavy, the former being carried in gaily-coloured carts drawn by horses, the latter on camelback.

Even in the infantry there were many French officers, for the service of the Mogul had then something of the same attraction for adventure-loving younger sons as service in the Varangian Guard had for the English of the eleventh century. These French officers soon made their fortune, for they were far better paid than the infantry officers of any European army. Their duties were light. As one of them told Dr. Careri: "*Le service du Mogul n'est qu'un plaisir et un jeu.*" Even the private soldiers were subjected to little discipline; the worst punishment, even for disobedience or desertion, was a fine or a reduction in pay.

[1] Manucci, during Jai Sing's campaign against Shivaji, received, as officer in charge of the artillery, three hundred rupees a month. As a regular salary, this was enviable, considering the purchasing power of money then, and is comparable to the salaries of Byzantine officers.

A vast number of camp followers accompanied the army, together with the relations and friends of the soldiers. Manucci noted that almost every soldier had with him his wife and children. "Thus," he wrote, "a soldier may be seen carrying under his arm an unweaned infant and on his head a basket of cooking-pots and pans. Behind him marches his wife with his spears or else matchlock upon her back. In place of a bayonet they stick into the muzzle of the gun a spoon, which, being long, is more conveniently carried there than in the basket borne by the husband upon his head." Many of the gentlemen who rode with the army were courtiers with little interest in the campaign. They would never, Dr. Careri wrote, use a musket, "*par la peur qu'ils ont de bruler leur grande barbe.*" But beside these exquisites marched bands of savage Pathan and Arab mercenaries.

On a campaign the pomp of the Mogul commander-in-chief was as great as that of the Emperor at Delhi. Aurangzeb's tent was surrounded by a hundred lackeys with gold staves, and he was attended by nine aides-de-camp in velvet and cloth of gold with huge puffed sleeves and collars with long points hanging down behind to the waist. If his private life was as austere as a monk's Aurangzeb never failed to maintain the dignity of his position by the outward display of majesty. Round his quarters stood a rank of elephants bearing standards and banners. When he left his tent he was saluted by trumpeters blowing on green trumpets eight feet long. These instruments emitted a curious booming roar which reminded the irreverent Dr. Careri of the noises which "*les porcherons font en Italie, lorsque la nuit ils veulent rassembler leurs cochons égarez.*" (sic).

Shivaji offered no resistance to the advance of Aurangzeb's army. He had declared himself a feudatory of the Empire, so that he had no cause to complain at the use of his territories by the Imperial forces; and any overt resistance would have been useless; a long time had to pass before he could challenge the full strength of the Empire. He retired into the mountains and waited while the Imperial troops marched down on either side of his bridge of hill-forts, down the Deccan Plateau and the coastland. Perhaps from some lookout on a granite cliff he watched the procession of camels with the guns jolting down the dusty roads, the war-elephants, the pointed helmets and plumed lances of the Mogul cavalry and the Tartar horse-tail banners streaming in the clear February air. Kalyan, whose capture had been Shivaji's first signal success, was prudently abandoned by the Marathas, and a Muhammadan, though now Imperialist, governor ruled once more in the old palace. Steadily the Mogul army pushed south.

In despair, Ali of Bijapur offered his submission

in terms of servile humility. He sent messenger after messenger with new proposals. But Aurangzeb received their petitions with a pitiless smile. It was no increase of territory for the Empire he desired, no new treaty with elaborate protestations of submission to Delhi. He wanted to destroy that centre of heresy, that unrighteous city of the plain.

It was useless to resist the Moguls in the field. The people of Bijapur burnt their crops, deserted their fields and villages and streamed into the great city, to seek refuge behind those enormous walls. Suppliants lay prostrate in the Mosques, before the tombs of old kings (those lovely tombs with painted convolvulus flowers and carved pen-cases) in the Shrine of the Relic of the Prophet's Hairs, beating their breasts and knocking their foreheads on the pavement under the simpering grimaces of Italian amoretti and the indifferent smiles of those languorous Venuses of the ceiling frescoes. Sorcerers, ancestors of those southern wizards whom Tipu enlisted to further his cause against the English, prepared their spells and maledictions. And along the walls the famous old Turkish guns, revered as almost divine, were stripped of their carpets and cloth of gold and made ready for battle. The gaping jaws of the Monarch of the Plain were crammed with sackfuls of stones and sharp nails and broken glass. Smoke-grimed gunners worked naked to the waist under the noon sun.

What the villagers had abandoned in their flight Aurangzeb destroyed with malignant ingenuity; trees, orchards and gardens were burnt; canals filled with earth and fields sown with salt. In his plain white tunic, one hand on his sword-hilt, the other holding to his thin nose a rose-petal, Aurangzeb gazed on the city spread before him, already in his grasp.

Meanwhile Shivaji, though safe in his mountain refuge, became impatient at his present inactivity. He could not resist the excitement of a little raid in the Mogul rear. If this raid would appear foolhardy and unnecessary, its success is some justification. Till now his cavalry had been mounted on the small shambling ponies that the hillmen use on their steep paths. If his mounted arm was ever to compete with that of the Moguls—with their traditions of horsemanship inherited from the lightning campaigns of their Mogul ancestors, and with the irregular forces of their Rajput tributaries—he must somehow provide his cavalry with better mounts than their present ones. So with a few hundred men Shivaji rode over the Mogul border, and pounced upon Ahmednagar, the capital of the frontier province. He could not hope to hold the place, but he carried off from Aurangzeb's own stables a thousand cavalry mounts and returned to his hills in safety.

The news of this impudent raid was carried to

Aurangzeb in his camp before the walls of Bijapur. In icy rage he wrote to his subordinates, censuring their negligence. The harsh, schoolmasterish rebukes were followed by directions for the punishment to be inflicted on Shivaji; his lands were to be occupied at once by Mogul troops, who should "lay waste the villages and kill the people without pity." All the Mogul officers and all the villagers living in the territory through which Shivaji passed on his raid must also be executed for not having resisted the passage of the Marathas with greater vigour; the fact that the Marathas reached Ahmednagar at all argued a disloyalty and incapacity among the local officials that could only be expiated by their death.

The breaking of the monsoon prevented these comprehensive measures of revenge being carried out at once; and in the interval Shivaji—having obtained as many cavalry mounts as he needed for the moment, but also requiring above all things time to train his men—wrote to Aurangzeb, imploring pardon and offering submission and reparation.

Aurangzeb would have treated these messages as he treated those from Bijapur, but before the end of the monsoon the Emperor Shah Jehan had fallen ill at Delhi. His death was hourly expected, and the Prince Imperial, Dara, began to act as regent in anticipation of his early succession to the throne.

Alone of the Princes of the Blood, Aurangzeb

had an army on a war footing. He refused to accept Dara's self-assumed regency. He raised the siege of Bijapur and marched northwards, granting to Bijapur terms of unhoped-for clemency. But as he went northward that December, he wrote to his officers on the border, instructing them to keep a watch on Shivaji's movements. "Attend to this"—and behind the precise words one can almost hear the sharp, cold voice. "Attend to this, for that son of a dog is only waiting his chance."

During all the next year Northern India was thrown into confusion by the War of Succession. Aurangzeb, who was never happy unless he had convinced himself of the rectitude of his actions, probably sincerely believed that under the rule of Dara, who was known to have Christian sympathies,[1] the supremacy of Islam in India would be endangered. Actually the story he put about, and which he must have known to be untrue, was that Dara had caused Shah Jehan's illness by poisoning his food. Too shrewd at once to advance his own claims, Aurangzeb declared for his elder brother Prince Murad, Governor of Gujarat, as Regent. Murad was also championed by Prince Shuja, Governor of Bengal. Unfortunately Shah Jehan

[1] He had been under instruction from the Flemish Jesuit, Buzée. But at the same time he studied Hinduism with sympathy and translated into Persian the sacred Upanishads of the Hindus, and wrote a work in which he attempted to reconcile Hinduism and Islam by naming it somewhat portentously *The Mingling of Two Oceans*.

suddenly recovered and ordered his sons to return to their duties. They refused to obey and marched on the capital. Aurangzeb had already begun to prejudice Murad against Shuja by insisting on the latter's heretical views. "As for myself," he added, "I have only one desire, to see an orthodox Emperor installed and then I shall gladly end my days as an anchorite."

The Imperial Court was torn by the intrigues and manœuvres of the Emperor's two daughters, Jehanara and Roshanara. The former, her father's favourite, was very beautiful; a scholar and poetess; devoted to her brother Dara with whom she used to study the Persian poets and discuss the verses of the great contemporary mystic Tabrizi, whose philosophy can be summed up in his well-known utterance, "All this talk of religion and infidelity finally leads to one place, the dream is the same dream, only the interpretations differ." Roshanara had none of her sister's beauty but she consoled herself with adopting a way of life of almost fantastic pomp and luxury; always conscious of the greater favour her sister enjoyed not only with their father but with all the Court she made herself feared for her bitter tongue and her vitriolic wit; jealous of her brother Dara's charm she was a passionate adherent of Aurangzeb and her intrigues often paralysed the Emperor's policy. Unceasingly she represented Aurangzeb as a misunderstood and loyal son, a staunch Muslim, a fit heir to the throne.

At last, however, Shah Jehan declared all his three younger sons to be rebels and put them under the ban of the Empire. The Prince Imperial, Dara, was appointed to command the loyal forces. When he came to take leave of his father the old man clung to him and wept bitterly, begging him to take care of himself. Dara said with Spartan brevity, "The Throne or the Tomb," rode out and was defeated. The rebel princes entered Agra and deposed Shah Jehan. He was imprisoned in the fort, where the lovely Jehanara shared his captivity while Roshanara rode exultantly beside Aurangzeb.

Then Aurangzeb invited Prince Murad to dinner, made him drunk, and bribed a slave girl, under pretence of amorous caresses, to remove his sword. Aurangzeb's guards fell on the unarmed Prince, who was shackled with golden chains and hurried away through the night. Next morning Aurangzeb proclaimed himself Emperor. A few months later Dara was executed. He had asked to be allowed to see the Jesuit, Buzée, and be received as a Catholic, but this was not allowed. Dara said "Muhammad has destroyed me but the Son of God and Mary will give me life," and awaited his execution with calm. His head was brought on a silver dish to Aurangzeb who prodded it with the point of his sword and began to jeer at the dead man. Then he had the head packed and sent to his father, Shah Jehan was at first deeply touched that his son had sent him a present and began eagerly to unpack the parcel; but when he found what the parcel contained he fell down in a dead faint.

As a final humiliation to the dead Prince, Aurangzeb decided to possess his wife Ra-na-dil, a Hindu courtesan with whom Dara had fallen so deeply in love as to marry her and persuade his father to create her a Princess of the House of Tamerlane. When summoned to the Imperial harem Ra-na-dil returned a message to Aurangzeb, "The beauty you have desired exists no longer; if my blood can gratify you, it is yours," and taking a dagger she stabbed herself repeatedly in the face.

The long drama of this civil war concluded with the beheading of Murad, the flight of Shuja into Burma where he was killed, and the slow murder of Dara's son, Sulaiman, who was forced to drink daily an infusion of poppies which reduced him gradually to torpor, to imbecility, to paralysis and to a frightful death—only such deliberate and feline cruelty could satisfy Aurangzeb's passionate resentment against his brilliant elder brother, the heretic and poet and tragic jester who had mocked at him and dubbed him "that prayer monger."[1]

[1] For these events, Manucci; and also Bernier's *History of the Late Rebellion in the States of the Great Mogol.*

CHAPTER NINE

UNHOPED for deliverance from Aurangzeb put new life and spirit into the Bijapur government. It must have been clear that some day or other the Mogul would return, but as long as the War of Succession lasted, Bijapur would have respite. The Queen-Mother, who on the death of the late Sultan emerged as the dominating character of the court, a woman of intelligence and vigour and far more ruler of Bijapur than her nineteen-year-old son, pressed on the ministers the necessity of subduing the various vassals of the State whose insubordination had facilitated the Mogul advance. The foremost of these vassals was, of course, Shivaji. From now on he was almost an obsession with the Bijapur court. In Dr. Fryer's words, they "reckoned him as a diseased Limb, impostulate and swollen too big for the Body; prejudicial in being his own Paymaster, rewarding himself most unconscionably . . . an Inhuman Butcherly Fellow."

Early in 1659 the Queen-Mother called on the nobles of her court to volunteer for service in an army which should finally crush Shivaji and restore the old boundaries of the State. The first to volunteer was her own brother-in-law, Afzul Khan, an Afghan of great height and enormous strength, a successful general and a fearless swordsman who had distinguished himself in feats of arms against the Moguls during the recent siege. Under his command a large army was assembled, equipped with Turkish artillery. In open court Afzul Khan indulged in frantic boasting; he would take the wretched Hindu bandit prisoner without even troubling to dismount from his horse; he would put him in a cage like the rat he was and bring him to the capital for the mob to jeer at. But in private conversation he was less confident. He consulted the Queen-Mother who advised him to capture Shivaji by pretending friendship.

Reflecting on Afzul Khan's fate a Muhammadan historian was moved to exclaim, "The Angel of Death led him by the collar to his doom"; and indeed over all these preliminaries to the campaign there broods an atmosphere of nightmare and dread. According to Maratha tradition, when Afzul Khan went to pray in the great Mosque to obtain a blessing for his enterprise, the officiating priest recoiled in horror from him, crying out that he had no head upon his shoulders, only a gaping hollow and a bleeding trunk. Aware that this omen portended his death, Afzul Khan returned to his palace, whose melancholy ruins may still be seen, a vast grey pile on the outskirts of the city. There he ordered all the sixty-four women of his harem to be drowned so that they should not submit to the embrace of a stranger after his end. Uncomplaining and resigned, all but one of his women went to their death; but the sixty-fourth tried to run away and was cut down. To-day the visitor is shown the sixty-three little graves set close together in rows and, at a little distance, the sixty-fourth grave where the poor last wife's attempt at escape ended.

Spurned to frenzy by further omens, Afzul Khan set out with his army. His advance into the Maratha country was attended with awful cruelty. Apparently he hoped either to terrify his opponents into submission or else to draw down Shivaji out of his mountains in fury. Hindu temples were torn down, their images pounded to dust, sacred cattle slaughtered and their blood dashed upon the altars. In the intervals between such violent activities Afzul Khan amused himself constructing an ingeniously uncomfortable cage in which he proposed to lodge Shivaji.

In Shivaji's camp the news of Afzul Khan's approach, of his boasts and of his cruelties, at first filled the Marathas with alarm. Hitherto they had only engaged in surprise raids on ill-defended towns or on carelessly-guarded forts in their own hill country. But now a great army—Arab cavalry, Afghan and Pathan infantry, Turkish artillery—was moving with terrifying deliberation against them. The confidence which Shivaji's successes had roused in them now ebbed away. At a council of war all Shivaji's staff clamoured against a battle and urged Shivaji to get what terms he could. Shivaji was ready to negotiate. No one could distract a ponderous Mussulman noble better than he with thin-spun webs of diplomatic courtesy. But he realised that until his Marathas faced the Muhammadans in battle they would never be really independent. All night the council wrangled. Shivaji left it for a few hours' sleep in the early hours of the morning. It is said that his resolution was confirmed by a dream. With courage renewed Shivaji returned to the council and insisted on hostilities. His officers agreed, but reluctantly, convinced of inevitable disaster. Then he sent word to his mother. That indomitable woman journeyed at once to his camp in the hills. When she learned his decision to resist at all costs she nodded and told him that no other course was open to him now.

At this point an unexpected embassy arrived from Afzul Khan offering attractive terms; if Shivaji would only make a nominal act of submission to Bijapur, the Sultan would recognise his claim to effective control of the territories already held. Shivaji, who naturally knew nothing of the Queen-Mother's advice to capture him by treachery, must have been astonished at such proposals after Afzul Khan's tremendous boasts and the much-advertised cage and the instances of calculated frightfulness. But he concealed his suspicions and entertained the envoys with flattering attentions. Now one of these envoys was a Brahman.[1] That night Shivaji crept into his tent and, throwing himself on the Brahman's mercy, begged him, if he were a true Hindu, if he recalled the age-old honour of his high caste, to tell him truthfully what lay behind the Khan's sudden proposals. The Brahman hesitated for a while, realising what punishments awaited him if Afzul Khan learnt of his breach of confidence. Shivaji reminded him of the temples Afzul Khan had destroyed during his advance, of the idols defaced and the shrines defiled. The Brahman gave way. He said he knew nothing himself, but he had heard the Khan's staff discussing the proposed offer of terms; they mentioned that it was hoped to secure the rebel's person by luring him to a peace conference.

Shivaji thanked the Brahman, promised him a great reward in land after the war and begged of him yet one more favour. Would he, on his return, tell the Khan that Shivaji was out of his mind with terror; and that while longing to submit he dared not descend to the Khan's camp . . . and then a suggestion . . . would not the Khan, who was known to be as brave as a lion, come to meet Shivaji?

[1] One of the factors advantageous to Shivaji in his struggle with the Muhummadan states was that Hindu officials in those states would be bound to be sympathetic to his cause. The rise of Clovis in Europe offers a parallel. The Franks, though numerically inferior to the Gothic kingdoms, could, as Catholics, count on the sympathy of a majority of the Gothic rulers' subjects who were Catholics.

The next day the envoys returned and Afzul Khan listened complacently to the Brahman's account of Shivaji's fears. Of course he would meet Shivaji wherever he wished. The Brahman suggested, as a suitable rendezvous, the crest of a hill under the high fort of Pratapgad which Shivaji had built with More's treasure. It was an open plateau, overlooking the Koyna valley. It was surrounded by thick jungle of which only Shivaji's hillmen knew the mazy paths.

Shivaji set his men to clear a road to this plateau through the brushwood and thickets. The road led just to the plateau and stopped there. Unless one knew the forest paths there was no way of return from the plateau except by this same road. In the jungle on either side Shivaji posted his men, invisible to any one unaccustomed to the uncertain light and shadow of the forests. He spent the night before the interview with Afzul Khan prostrate in a temple of the Mother-Goddess; the vigil of the warrior before the crisis of his life. At dawn he rose and performed the ritual ablutions as though for a day of high festival. He breathed a prayer to the Earth-Goddess and begged her to bear him firmly that day. Raising his face to the sun he cast before him a libation of cold spring water, the drops sparkling in the clear mountain air, as he called upon the Sun-god, the Creator. Then he put on a white tunic; but under it he wore a coat of mail. In his belt he thrust a dagger wrought like a scorpion and in the palm of his left hand he clasped a small but terrible weapon, the *wag-nak*, a row of sharp steel claws, supposed to represent the claws of a tiger.[1]

He had no illusions about his peril; to his officers he commended his family if he perished. He made careful provision for the succession to his leadership, for the administration of his estates and the command of his men. As he stood on a wild eminence of the hills, his officers round him, their faces darkened with foreboding, his mother Jijabai came suddenly out of the forest. Like her son she was dressed in spotless white. The long robes gave her the air of a priestess. She walked with head erect and eyes shining. Shivaji left his officers and ran to her. He knelt before her and touched her feet. For a while they were motionless against the sky, the kneeling soldier and his mother, the officers standing silent with heads averted. A moment of tension and suspense on that lonely hill, round which the vultures circled slowly. Jijabai broke the silence. Laying her hand on Shivaji's head she blessed him. She began, "Victory shall be yours. . . ." But the proud phrases required by the epic occasion faltered; finally, it was a frail sad voice that murmured, "Be careful, my son, ah, be careful."

Meanwhile in Afzul Khan's camp trumpet and

[1] This weapon is shown to visitors to the temple of the Mother Goddess in Satara to-day.

kettledrum and gong welcomed the day. Cavalry and artillery advanced slowly over the lower foothills. Even on this morning omens pursued Afzul Khan. The leading elephant, bearing the crescent banner of Bijapur, suddenly stopped, trembling; no effort of its mahout could induce it to advance. Like some tyrant of Greek tragedy, a Pentheus heedless of heaven's warnings, Afzul Khan drove onward to his doom. He had Shivaji in his grasp. Already he pictured to himself a triumphal return to Bijapur, the flag-decked streets and carpet-hung balconies. He hastened on ahead of his army in a palanquin attended by two bodyguards and a giant swordsman named Bandu.

By the terms of the interview, Afzul Khan and Shivaji were each to be accompanied by three men only. Afzul Khan rightly estimated that his own strength together with that of his swordsmen would be more than a match for anything that Shivaji could produce. Exulting he hastened towards the place of meeting, guided by the Brahman envoy he had sent to Shivaji. They passed along the road Shivaji had had cut through the forest, watched by hundreds of eyes. If he heard a crack of dry twigs he must have assumed that some wild creature had darted back into safety from the noise of men.

At the meeting place a great tent had been erected, furnished with carpets and silken cushions. Afzul Khan entered the tent with his followers. Shivaji approached and then, seeing the swordsman Bandu, stopped dead. Why did the Bijapur embassy need a noted swordsman in its train, he inquired. He offered to dismiss one of his own attendants if only Afzul Khan would leave Bandu outside the tent. Afzul Khan agreed. Then Shivaji entered the tent. Afzul Khan seemed determined to pick a quarrel at once. Without even referring to the purpose of his mission he began loudly to complain that it was intolerable to find a petty landowner's son aping the airs of a prince, furnishing a tent so luxuriously. Shivaji replied that the cushions and carpets were there not for his own comfort but as a compliment to the distinguished envoy from Bijapur. For the moment Afzul Khan seemed satisfied. He nodded slowly and opened his arms to offer Shivaji the embrace customarily exchanged between opposing leaders at a peace conference. Shivaji stepped forward to accept the embrace. He was more than a head shorter than Afzul Khan. As soon as they were locked in an embrace the Khan moved his arm up Shivaji's back and clutched him round the neck. It was a wrestler's grip. As soon as Shivaji felt that strong arm close suddenly upon his neck he felt faint with sudden fear.[1] He wriggled in the Muhammadan's grasp but the grip only tightened. He would have been swung clear off his feet had he

[1] So he told Ramdas afterwards. Hanmant's Life of Ramdas quoted in Kincaid and Parasnis.

not with a sudden snake-like movement twisted round, got his right arm free and dug the steel tiger-claws concealed in the palm of his left hand deep into Afzul Khan's back. Then with his right hand he drew his scorpion dagger from his belt and drove it into Afzul Khan's side. The Afghan staggered back, shouting with rage and pain. His attendants came running up; as did also Shivaji's. There was a short duel between the two parties; but the Muhammadans were hampered by their desire to get their wounded leader away to his camp. They carried him to his palanquin, parrying the blows of the Marathas as they ran. The Marathas slashed at their legs to make them drop their burden. Shivaji and one of his attendants cut down the great swordsman, Bandu. One by one the other attendants of Afzul Khan were wounded or killed. Then a Maratha cut off Afzul Khan's head and lifted it up in triumph.

Shivaji stopped and blew his horn. In the narrow defiles of the hills, from cliff and scarp, it echoed and re-echoed. The Marathas concealed in the labyrinth of the forest heard it and seized their arms. From the Fort of Pratapgad, overlooking the scene of the meeting, a great gun boomed. Trumpets roared a battle-pæan and, lance in rest, the Marathas poured through the woods to fling themselves on the Muhammadans among the foothills. The main body of the Bijapur army was still ignorant of the fate of Afzul Khan. Many of the horsemen had dismounted to rest in the shade; the guns were unmanned and the sentries nodding. The Maratha attack was a complete surprise. Horse and foot were swept away in confusion. Camels plunged panic-stricken through the ranks. War elephants trumpeted dismally, uncertain and alarmed, till the Marathas dashed at them, hacked at their legs and trunks and sent them stumbling in terror through the jungle. The Bijapur captains were helpless to arrest the rout. Their voices were drowned in the tumult. They were whirled away in the torrent of their fleeing army. Whole companies were dispersed over the hills, returning days later in twos and threes, starving and distraught, to throw themselves on Shivaji's mercy.

Even at this delirious moment of victory Shivaji's orders were obeyed. All who surrendered were spared. All women and children, priests, camp-followers and non-combatants were sent to their homes in safety. Even the captive soldiers were not retained. Officers and men alike were brought before Shivaji, who sympathised with them in their misfortune, loaded them with money, food and clothing and set them free.

Clement to the defeated enemy, Shivaji was munificent to his own victorious troops. So immense was the booty that he could afford to be generous. All the Bijapur artillery ammunition, transport animals, luggage and treasure had fallen into his hands; four thousand horses and sixty-five elephants and twelve hundred camels. To the widows of the Marathas who had fallen, Shivaji allotted pensions; to the wounded, prizes of treasure; to the officers who had distinguished themselves, elephants, jewels and robes of honour.

When the news of the rout reached Bijapur there was consternation and bitter grief. The whole court went into mourning. The Queen-Mother shut herself in a room and refused to eat or drink. She only emerged from her seclusion to go on pilgrimage to Mecca.

For the moment it seemed as if even Bijapur City itself would fall to the Marathas and the panic that reigned there was as great as at the approach of the Moguls. But there was no chance that where the siege-engines of Aurangzeb had failed Shivaji's hillmen would succeed. Moreover, though Bijapur was never again able to challenge Shivaji's independence, her wealth now saved her from further humiliation. She could buy armies and artillery to replace those that had been lost. New regiments of mercenaries were recruited and a capable Abyssinian condottiere, Sidi Johar, was given command of the army. Shivaji, who had ventured with insufficient forces into the heart of Bijapur territory, was surprised by Sidi Johar and retreating to Panhala was there invested. Once again he resorted to diplomacy. He offered to surrender—but on the following day. It is almost incredible that the Muhammadans should have paid serious attention to this obviously frivolous offer; but apparently they did, for they agreed to the proposal. And of course, in the night, the investing forces having relaxed their vigilance in anticipation of the morrow's armistice, Shivaji slipped out of the town with a few followers and galloped north to the defile of Rangana where there was a Maratha force.

Instead of pressing on the siege of Panhala, which in the absence of Shivaji would probably have capitulated, the Abyssinian, furious at the trick played on him, raised the siege and followed Shivaji to Rangana. The body of Marathas posted at Rangana was far too small to engage the whole Bijapur army with any possibility of success. But while Shivaji continued his retreat to join the main Maratha army many miles to the rear, he gave the command of the Rangana force to Baji Prashu (who had formerly been steward to More) and ordered him to hold the defile till he heard a gunshot which would announce Shivaji's safe arrival.

Baji had only a few hundred hillmen to defend the pass with. He made them pile up a barricade of stones across the mouth of the defile. Behind this they awaited the Muhammadan attack. All day the heavy cavalry of Bijapur dashed against the band of hillmen who, falling one by one, never retreated by one step from the position Shivaji had ordered them to hold. Their commander, Baji, was desperately wounded; but even as he lay in agony he cried out continual encouragement to his men. Towards evening when there seemed no hope of further resistance, they heard the distant boom of a gun that told them Shivaji was safe. Bearing their dying commander on a rude stretcher, the Marathas fell back from the defile, not even molested in their retreat by the exhausted enemy.

The defence of Rangana has become legendary in Western India. The action is remarkable as an example of the spirit which Shivaji's leadership had infused into his followers. A band of despised hillmen, of Hindus hitherto resigned to submission, had stood up to the attack of vastly superior forces in the manner of Spartiates.

The war thereafter languished. It was obvious that Bijapur would never be able to subdue Shivaji; nor could the Marathas at this stage hope to take Bijapur. But the power of Bijapur was broken and Shivaji was willing to make peace on condition of the recognition of his independence. Negotiations for permanent peace were opened in 1662. The envoy chosen by the Bijapur government was Shivaji's own father, Shahaji.

Shahaji had neglected and disliked his son during

his childhood; a troublesome, pigheaded boy had grown up into a wild rebel whose activities had led to his father's imprisonment; but now the difficult child had become a conqueror and independent prince, a hero to his fellow countrymen.

The meeting between father and son must have been curious. They had not met since Shivaji was nineteen. Now he was a warrior of note, his face already lined and hardened. Instead of the rustic tunic he wore when Jijabai brought him to Bijapur he was clothed now like a prince. For all his father's former indifference to him Shivaji treated the old man with wonderful courtesy. As a boy he had refused to bow before the Sultan of Bijapur; but now that he was more feared than the Sultan, he approached his father with hands clasped humbly under his chin, prostrated himself at full length and laid his forehead upon his father's feet. Bursting into tears Shahaji raised his son and embraced him. Shivaji had ordered a palanquin of princely magnificence for his father but he himself walked barefoot beside the palanquin. He led his father to a great pavilion where a banquet was prepared; but he refused to sit at meat with his father, contenting himself with standing meekly before him with arms crossed upon his breast. Shahaji begged him to sit beside him. Shivaji replied, "Not till you have forgiven me for having been the cause of your imprisonment by the Sultan." Once again Shahaji wept and begged his son to forget the past. So they were reconciled and sat down to the banquet together.

Shahaji had been given full powers as plenipotentiary by the Bijapur government. All Shivaji's demands were met. His independence was conceded and he was recognised as ruler of all the coast territory from Bombay to Goa, of all the forts that he had captured and of the Deccan plateau as far East as Indapur.

When this treaty was concluded Shahaji returned to Bijapur and resumed office under the Sultan. He never saw his son again. He was killed not long after in an accident in the hunting field.

PART THREE

CHIEFTAIN

CHAPTER TEN

BEFORE peace with Bijapur was concluded Shivaji first made acquaintance with the English. Two years before that peace the English had acquired Bombay from the Portuguese. The headquarters of the East India Company was still at Surat where permission to settle and trade had been granted by the Emperor Jehangir in 1608. In 1615 Sir Thomas Roe had visited the Mogul Court and, greatly impressing the Emperor by his integrity and courage,[1] had won a new respect for the English. English seamanship was becoming famous in Indian waters. But the English were still traders without pretensions or ambitions. So it was unwise of the English factors at Rajapur to supply Bijapur with artillery to replace the guns lost with Afzul Khan. It was even less prudent of some English clerks, tired of ledgers and lists of sales of pepper and cardamum, to accompany that artillery to amuse themselves by "tossing Balls with a Flag that was known to be the English's" into the Maratha camp at Panhala just before Shivaji's precipitate retreat to Rangana.

[1] The Empress, however, could not resist teasing the solemn priggish foreigner. She sent a female slave to await him in his bed. Fortunately perhaps for Sir Thomas' virtue, the charmer was but "a grave woeman of forty years."

Not unnaturally Shivaji was incensed and in December, 1660, he fell upon Rajapur and carried away four of the factors. They were kept prisoners for about three years, Shivaji claiming damages from the Company for their servants' breach of neutrality and the company claiming compensation for the destruction of their warehouses at Rajapur.

The four captives were well-treated but found their confinement irksome and made an abortive attempt to escape. The Council at Surat fulminated against "that Grand Rebell, Sevajee" and lamented that they could not call him to account, "because they had not either conveniency of Force or Time." But when the prisoners grew impatient and sent a rude letter to the Council at Surat, urging them to take more interest in their case and get them released, the Council fell into a temper with the wretched factors (whom they had hitherto addressed as "loving brethren") and wrote sharply, "How you came in Prison you know very well. 'Twas not for defending the Company's goods; 'twas for going to the siege of Panhala."

Shivaji released his captives without ransom after he had signed the treaty with Bijapur. But the Company continued to press for compensation. Shivaji received each successive envoy with courtesy —even seating one, Mr. Nicholls, on his throne beside him—but refused to return more than vague counter-proposals. In vain the Council deplored his

"Subtility, Self-policy and insecure Inconstancy" and talked of reprisals. But Shivaji never paid the compensation demanded. It is difficult to blame him.

In spite of periods of official coldness between Shivaji and the Company, the English were increasingly impressed by Shivaji's qualities. When Aurangzeb turned his attention to crushing the Marathas, most observers predicted an early collapse of the new state; but the English governor of Bombay considered Mogul success improbable. "'Tis well known," he wrote, "that Sevagy is a second Sertorious and comes not short of Hannibal for Stratagems." And presently "that Grand Rebell" is referred to with half-amused admiration as "our old and dear friend Sevajy."

The four factors from Rajapur had been imprisoned at Raigad; and during their captivity Shivaji was fortifying this place and preparing it to be his capital. This was the greatest of all his forts, and even to-day the visitor gains an impression of its former grandeur. Dr. Fryer, describing the adventures of the 1673 embassy, wrote of it, "It is fortified by nature rather than Art, there being one Avenue to it, which is guarded by two narrow Gates, and fortified by a strong wall exceeding high and Bastions thereto. On the Mountain are many strong Buildings, as the *Rajah's* court and the houses of other Ministers. . . ." Proceeding to the Palace the envoys saw "the Rajah seated on a Magnificent throne and all his Nobles waiting on him in Rich Attire, the rest, as well Officers of the Army as others, standing with great Respect. The English made their obeisance at a distance. . . . He (Shivaji) presently took notice of it and ordered their coming nearer, even to the Foot of the Throne, where being vested, they were desired to retire; which they did not do so soon, but they took notice on each side of the Throne there hung on heads of Gilded Launces many Emblems of Dominion and Government; as on the Right-hand were two great Fishes Heads of Gold, with very large Teeth, on the Left, several Horses Tails, a Pair of Gold Scales, on a very high Launces head, equally poized, an Emblem of Justice; and as they returned, at the Palace Gate, stood two small Elephants on each side, and two Fair Horses with Gold Trappings, Bridles and Rich furniture: which made them admire how they brought them up the Hill, the Passage being both difficult and hazardous."

The pomp at this reception should not, however, be taken as evidence of a ripening appetite for the appurtenances of royalty; it was maintained chiefly for the benefit of foreigners and visitors from other states. Ordinarily the Court of Shivaji was distinguished by most un-Oriental simplicity. As Mr. Orme learned with surprise, "his life was simple even to parsimony; his manners void of insolence or ostentation; as a sovereign most humane and solicitous for the well-being of his people . . . the same principles of frugality and expense were observed in the municipal disbursements of his government; far superior himself to magnificence, none of his officers were led to expect more than competence. In personal activity he exceeded all of whom there is record. He met every emergency . . . with instant discernment and unshaken fortitude. . . . Respected as the guardian of the nation he had founded he moved everywhere amongst them with unsuspicious security and often alone."

He was far less at home in his palace than among his soldiers, and the cultured Dr. Fryer said, "This Barbarian Commander is like the Scythian Ateas, who hearing one sweetly modulating on the Ismean Pipe, swore he had rather hear the neighing of an Horse or the Clangour of Horses or Trumpets." In presenting him as a philistine, if pleasant mannered, soldier Fryer naturally took no account of Shivaji's deep attachment to his religion and his great love of poetry. That devotion to Tuharam's verse—those strange and almost overmastering onsets of religious fervour that many times in his life made Shivaji desire above all things to forsake the world and retire to the wilderness as a hermit—would hardly be known to a foreign visitor who only saw a lean, hawk-faced soldier with a sword at his belt and wide eager eyes and a smile lighting up his face whenever he spoke.

In contrast to the splendour of Shivaji's court on ceremonial occasions, the Maratha armies presented a disappointing spectacle. Fryer summed them up roundly as "Starved Rascals, accustomed to Fare Hard, Journey Fast and take little Pleasure." In fact, "they looked like our old *Britains*, half naked, and as Fierce." But the same critic admitted their superiority in some respects to the Mussulman armies in being "of a rougher Temper, more Hardy and less addicted to the soft vanities of Musick, Pomp or Stateliness." Unlike the soldiers of the Mogul armies they were subject to severe discipline, disobedience often entailing death. No women were allowed into the camp, nor was the wife or mistress of any soldier permitted to follow the armies on campaign. This wholesome provision, unprecedented in that age in Asia or (save for the New Model) in Europe, gave to Shivaji's forces a mobility hitherto unknown in Indian warfare.

For an impression of a Maratha camp on campaign we may return for a moment to the sensitive Captain Broughton[1] (whose comments on Maratha devotees of Comus will be remembered): "On marching days the quarter-master general moves off

[1] He is writing of more than a century after Shivaji's death, but the characteristics changed very little.

at an early hour; and, upon reaching the ground where the army is to encamp, he plants a small white flag, to mark the spot where the tents of the Muha Raj (commander) are to be pitched; and which collectively are termed the Deeoree. The flags of the different Bazars are then fixed as they arrive; always in the same situation to each other and in as straight a line as the ground will admit of. The shops for the troops' provisions called *Dokans*, are pitched in two lines running parallel to each other; and they form one grand street from the front to the rear of the army. The different chiefs encamp to the right and left of the principal street. . . . At the door of every tent is a fire, the smoke of which spreads throughout the whole camp; where it serves to keep the people warm, to drive the flies away from the cattle and to put out the eyes of all those who are unused to so gross an element."

The fastidious captain is describing the camp of a Maratha field-army at full strength. But in many of Shivaji's campaigns only cavalry were used and their bivouacs were very different. Speed was the main quality desired of the Maratha horsemen. An anonymous Englishman[1] writing in 1788, said that he had seen bodies of fifty to sixty thousand Maratha horse[2] advance across country for many days in succession at the rate of fifty miles a day.

[1] The author of *Present State of Native Powers in Hindustan*.

[2] In Shivaji's time, however, the Maratha forces seldom totalled more than 30,000.

The average mount was, he noticed, "a lean, ill-looking animal, but large-boned." His rider wore no defensive armour except a quilted jacket and "all his baggage and necessary food were contained in a small bag tied upon the saddle. The food of the rider consists in a few cakes already baked, a small quantity of flour and rice and some salt . . . that of the horses, balls of black peas mixed with garlick and hot spices. These balls they make use of by way of a cordial to restore the vigour of their horses after fatigue." In contrast to the infantry regiments, "tents are very rarely used by the cavalry. Even the officers have frequently nothing but a small carpet to sit and lie upon, and the whole baggage of the General is carried on one Camel. . . . The rider, having provided for his horse, sits down then to his own temperate meal, which having finished, he lies down perfectly contented by the side of his horse; and when called by the sound of the *Nagah*, or great Drum, is at once ready to mount." These great drums boomed out at dawn and in the thin mist the camp sprang to instant activity. A light meal was taken, the men squatting round a wood fire. In a short time the camp was broken up and the whole force had disappeared leaving hardly a trace of its bivouac. The same anonymous Englishman noted how fond the Marathas were of their horses and how cleverly they trained them. "By being constantly with their riders, who are fond of caressing and talking to them, they acquire the intelligence and docility of *more domestic* animals. They are taught to stop when in full gallop and to turn round instantly upon their hind legs as upon a pivot."

The cavalry arm was divided into Regulars and Irregulars. In the Regiments of Regulars the trooper was provided with a horse and received twelve rupees a month as pay. The Master of Horse received about eight hundred rupees. The Irregular Cavalry were less well paid and had to provide their own mounts. Rations were, both to Western and contemporary Mogul eyes, scanty. But then Shivaji himself only ate one meal a day.

The infantry was not provided with salaries but were paid in kind—all except Shivaji's Guard, composed of two thousand picked hillmen who were well paid and smartly uniformed.

There was nothing of the feudal levy or casual militia about Shivaji's army. Military service was regarded as a rare privilege and aspirants had to prove they were worthy of it. New soldiers were only admitted to the service after a personal interview with Shivaji and two soldiers already in Shivaji's employment had to stand surety for the recruit.

Throughout Shivaji's reign the Maratha forces were notably weak in artillery. They had a few light pieces of Indian manufacture but these were primitive in design and clumsy. They were described by a Dutch traveller as "made of long and broad

Bars of Iron, joined together with Iron Hoops." Shivaji relied largely on the Portuguese and English to provide him with artillery. The English generally began by protesting loudly that they could not possibly sell him any guns as that would amount to a breach of neutrality; but, finding the French and Portuguese less scrupulous and only too anxious to do a deal with the Marathas, they usually ended by supplying Shivaji with the guns he required and from 1670 onwards the Surat Factory records contain many references to sales of artillery to the Marathas. From an entry dated 1670 it would appear that English gunners sometimes accompanied the guns; for the factors in Bombay wrote advising Surat that "an Engineer and a great gun or two may be privately conveyed to him, Shivaji." Often, however, English scruples reasserted themselves and on one occasion it was necessary for Shivaji to send "an extraordinary kind letter to the President together with a present" before the promised guns were delivered. However, these guns were seldom worth the money paid for them and the English factors took a certain pleasure in recording the defects in the guns they had sold to the simple Marathas. Those despatched in 1671 are described as "very bad within, yet they may last a while"; those sold in 1672 as "old, defective guns with great holes in them"; and the 1673 consignment as "old and defective, many of them honey combe." Sometimes, too, the English, while promising to supply Shivaji with guns and even ships, left prematurely "A Hole to creep out of their Agreement" and broke their promises.

The military organisation of the new state was completed by a network of forts, some of them old forts built by Bijapur officers which Shivaji had captured and fortified anew and other forts which Shivaji himself constructed along strategic points of his dominions. Each fort was garrisoned by hillmen, under a Maratha commandant. The fort engineer was of the Prabhu caste and the civil officer a Brahman.[1] Outside each fort low-caste tribesmen were settled in newly-constructed villages to give warning of attack.

Of all his fortresses it was on Raigad, his capital, that Shivaji expended the most anxious care; desiring to make it impregnable. But when at last he flattered himself that the fortification was complete and that no human being could enter or leave the town except by the narrow gates of the single approach, a peasant woman showed him that his satisfaction was premature. She was called Hirakani and she used to visit Raigad daily to sell milk to the garrison. She lived in a village below the towering walls and she would return home at nightfall. But one evening she lingered later than usual in the fortress and when she reached the gates

[1] The point being, of course, the unlikelihood of collusion in treachery of men drawn from different castes.

she found them closed. In spite of her entreaties the sentries refused to let her out. At home she had a young child and the thought of leaving him alone and hungry all night nerved her to a feat of desperate courage. In the dark she climbed down the sheer face of the walls that Shivaji's practised eye had pronounced unscalable; and she reached home safely. When Shivaji heard of this he sent for the woman and rewarded her; and then built a tower to guard that sector of the battlements. In honour of the milk-women's courage he called it after her, the Hirakani Tower. Its ruins still bear the name.

CHAPTER ELEVEN

AURANGZEB had never forgotten Shivaji's raid in his rear during his advance on Bijapur. Now that he was undisputed Emperor and master of the vast resources of the Mogul dominions he decided to punish "that son of a dog." In 1663 he ordered south his uncle, Shayista Khan, Premier Peer of the Empire, with a hundred thousand cavalry, a regiment of Pathans and a great train of artillery. And so, hardly had Shivaji made his peace with Bijapur when he was forced to enter on a long struggle with the Great Mogul, a far more formidable adversary than Bijapur.

The Imperial Army entered Shivaji's territories towards the end of February. The Maratha forces, at this period, did not probably number more than ten thousand men, and a pitched battle in the plains with the Moguls was out of the question. Shivaji fell back towards the mountains, but his irregular horse hung on the flanks of the Imperialists, cutting off stragglers and raiding the baggage train. There were a few skirmishes between Mogul and Maratha cavalry in which the former were generally successful. The advance of the Mogul army continued without serious opposition, its pace only retarded by the weight of its enormous numbers. By May Poona was threatened and Shivaji had to abandon the town where he had passed his boyhood, the town which he had first seen deserted and in ruins and which under Dadaji's careful administration had proved so prosperous. So Shayista Khan entered Poona in triumph and concluded that already the first stage of the campaign was over. He had driven the Marathas into the hills and after the monsoon he would pursue them and stamp out their resistance. The monsoon broke early and immobilised military operations. Shayista chose for his quarters in Poona the Rang Mahal, or Painted Palace, which Dadaji had built for Shivaji and his mother on their return from Bijapur, and there with difficulty controlling his impatience, Shayista watched from the wide windows rain falling steadily on tile and thatch, churning the streets to mud and beating against the straw-hung walls of the palace.

His impatience overmastering his sense of dignity, he made a futile attempt to draw Shivaji from his hills by sending him a furious Persian couplet taunting him with the cowardice of a monkey, challenging him to come out of his hiding-place and fight like a man. Shivaji capped the couplet with one of his own in which he admitted possessing some monkey-like qualities but reminded Shayista that in Hindu legend monkeys had destroyed the prince of demons. This reply can hardly have soothed

Shayista's ill-temper, and he soon had cause to regret having invited Shivaji to leave his mountains.

In one of the Poona temples a famous minstrel was advertised to give a recital of Tukaram's poems. Shivaji heard of this. In spite of his continual and inevitable absorption in war he had never forgotten his meeting with that sweet singer. There came over him a sudden longing to hear again worthily sung those poems that always so moved him. Without a word to his officers he left his camp and reached the plains towards twilight.

The approaches to Poona were strongly guarded, for Shayista Khan for all his professed contempt for Shivaji's cowardice had heard enough of his "Stratagems" to take precautions against a sudden raid. But Shivaji evaded the guards and was in the city a few hours later. He went to the Temple where the recital was to be held and squatted down among the crowds in the temple courtyard. In the darkness, his head muffled with his turban, he was indistinguishable from his neighbours. But as he passed through the bazar some one had recognised him. Rumour took wings; everywhere Hindus whispered to each other that Shivaji was in the city. A band of Afghan mercenaries heard the story and surrounded the temple, probably already congratulating themselves on the rewards they would earn when they produced the captive Maratha before Shayista Khan.

In the temple the minstrel sang sitting cross-legged on a square stool as one may see minstrels still to-day singing Tukaram's poems in the Poona temples, his head silhouetted against the glow of the altar lamps, his right hand plucking at a stringed instrument laid across his knees. Then someone near the gateway gave the alarm. Afghans had surrounded the place. There was a moment of terror. Only Shivaji knew why the Afghans had come and knew that there would be no chance of escape for him. But he sat on. The recital came to an end. People began to whisper that the Afghans had gone. The temple courtyard emptied and in the long colonnades were only shadows and the uncertain light of torches burning low. Silence fell. Surprised at the respite Shivaji rose and went out into the street. There were no Afghans in sight.

According to Maratha tradition, at the very moment when the Afghans were about to rush the temple a muffled figure, apparently that of Shivaji, started out of a side door and ran down the street. The Afghans shouted, imagining that their prey was escaping. The figure ran on. The Afghans followed, racing up and down the streets and never gaining on the mysterious runner ahead. Whether it was chance, or whether (as Marathas like to think) a spirit had intervened to save him, Shivaji returned safe to his camp.

Soon after this exploit, Shivaji paid a second visit to Poona.

No Hindus might enter or leave Poona City and all the walls and gates were closely guarded day and night. But there were occasions when such restrictions might be waived. For instance, one had to discriminate between the Hindu soldiers serving with the Mogul standards and the native population of the town who might be justly suspected of an attachment to Shivaji. And when some Hindus in Imperial service presented themselves before the Mogul civil governor of Poona and begged permission for the marriage procession of a friend of theirs to enter the town in accordance with Hindu custom, the Governor felt that it would be unreasonable to refuse the request. Thanking him, the soldiers withdrew.

Towards evening the marriage party appeared at the gates, the young bridegroom riding ahead, dressed in a gold shawl, his head hung with chaplets of champak-blossom which concealed his features. Behind him walked musicians beating drums and playing pipes. Then followed the guests and friends of the bridegroom, gaily dressed for the occasion, laughing and talking. The sentries let the procession pass without suspicion.

A few minutes later appeared a band of Imperialist cavalry driving before them a number of Maratha prisoners whom they beat cruelly. The sentries shouted for news and were told of some skirmish—a Maratha attempt on the outposts or a Mogul raid into the hills—in which the Marathas after a feeble resistance had surrendered. The sentries laughed and congratulated the troopers who rode on into the town, their wearied prisoners stumbling before them.

It was soon night and the city gates were shut. In some secret quarter of the town, marriage procession, Imperialist troopers and Maratha prisoners met and threw off their disguises. They were, of course, Shivaji's men. Shivaji had himself approached the Governor and walked in the procession as a drummer. It was a dark night—"dark" wrote a chronicler, "as Shivaji's own heart." Presently rain began to fall, the heavy, steady rain of the monsoon. Shivaji led his men down the winding alleys of the poorer quarters till they came out near the river bank where Shivaji's old home, the Painted Palace, loomed up out of the night. They stood for a moment listening.

The river, swollen with monsoon torrents, ran tumultuously, rain hissing upon the dark flood. Any noise of the Marathas' approach would be drowned by the roar of the waters. No one seemed to be stirring in the Palace. There was no light nor any sound. If sentries had been posted they must have taken shelter from the rain. No challenge rang out as Shivaji climbed over the wall into the garden. Once within the Palace Shivaji had his enemy at a disadvantage; for he knew every yard of the building. He told most of his followers to wait in the garden and with twenty men he crept round to the main door. But there was a light there. Some eunuchs were drowsily gossiping. Shivaji moved like a shadow along the walls till he reached the kitchen door. Some cooks were preparing the dawn meal. The door was unlocked. Shivaji pushed it open noiselessly. The cooks, their backs to the door, were bending over their kitchen vessels. The Marathas sprang on the cooks, bore them to the ground and strangled them. It was over in a minute. Not a cry had been raised.

Now Shivaji remembered that only a clay wall separated the kitchen from the room where he had slept as a child, the chief room in the house, where Shayista Khan must now be sleeping. He told his men to bring tools from the garden and with spades and picks they attacked the wall. One of the Khan's servants was sleeping with his pallet against the wall and the dull thud of the pickaxes roused him. He ran to his master and awoke him. The Khan sat up in bed, rubbing his eyes and yawning. He was still heavy with sleep and impatient with the servant's suspicions. A noise in the kitchen? Well, it must be the cooks. He listened for a moment and heard a faint chock-chock. "That," he said angrily, "is only the noise made by the Horse Guards in the courtyard driving in pegs for their horses' heel-ropes."[1] Then he rounded on his servant and abused him for disturbing his rest with childish alarms. Grumbling, he lay down again and composed himself to sleep. A moment later the Marathas had made a breach in the wall. Shivaji, sword in hand, pushed his way through into the room and sprang towards the Khan's bed. With panic agility, Shayista rolled off his bed and Shivaji's stroke fell short, severing the Khan's thumb. The next moment a servant had dashed on to the floor the single lamp which dimly illumined the room, and in the darkness Shayista escaped into his harem where he hid among his slave-girls. Some Marathas stumbled after him and cut down two of the women without realising their sex. Shayista's son ran to his father's assistance and made a gallant stand before he was despatched; but his intervention gave his father time to escape; he was carried out of the Palace and hidden.

The whole Palace was now in an uproar. The eunuchs, screaming with fright, beat frantically on kettledrums to summon the Guard. But when the Guardsmen arrived no one could tell them where the enemy were, how many of them there were, or even *who* they were. The Guardsmen only added to the confusion as they plunged down the dark

[1] Manucci.

corridors, trampling upon terrified women and attacking the palace servants by mistake.

Meanwhile the remainder of Shivaji's force, which had remained behind in the garden, as soon as the alarm had been raised, rushed the front gateway, cutting down the sleepy sentries with joyous shouts of "What a way to keep guard!" While the main body poured into the palace, three or four Marathas dashed up the steps to the music-room over the gateway. There they roused the Khan's bandsmen and at the point of the sword made them take down their instruments from the walls and play merry tunes as loudly as they could. The deafening, but cheerful, noise not only added to the intolerable confusion but prevented the Mogul troops, who were gathering in bewilderment round the palace, from realising what was actually happening.

Meanwhile Shivaji had seen a Mogul noble trying to escape through a window. He took him to be Shayista Khan himself and ran him through. Then with extraordinary skill Shivaji collected his men, and leaving the Palace in pandemonium, ran by tortuous streets to the city gates. There they overpowered the sentries, Shivaji with a single stroke cutting off the trunk of a war-elephant with which the sentries tried to bar his path, opened the gates and escaped into the night.

Outside the city were the lines of ten thousand

Mogul heavy cavalry. When the news of Shivaji's raid reached their officers they gave the order to pursue and overtake the Marathas. Kettledrums roused the troopers from their tents. Soon a strong force rode out, following the road to the hills. Shivaji, foreseeing pursuit, had recourse to a "Stratagem." He halted his men in a copse through which the road passed and ordered them to tie lighted torches to every tree. When the Moguls saw the blaze of torches across their path they drew rein and consulted together. Believing that the whole Maratha army must be encamped only a few hundred yards ahead they did not venture to attack but retired to Poona to report.

Shayista Khan's reason appears to have been affected by Shivaji's raid. When his staff called on him in the morning to condole with him on the loss of his thumb, he remained silent, biting his lips with fury. Suddenly his eyes fell on the Maharaja of Jodhpur, who had accompanied the Mogul Army as a loyal feudatory of the Empire, and he burst out, accusing the Rajput prince of cowardice and negligence, "When the enemy fell upon me, did you forget that you were in the service of His Majesty?" The Rajput turned away and left the palace in a rage. Then with an ill-assorted force, without any artillery (which the rain, still falling heavily, would have made almost impossible to move) Shayista Khan moved towards the hills. He made no attempt to reconnoitre the ground and some Maratha gunners, having concealed their artillery in some brushwood, were able to wait till the vanguard of the Mogul force was within a few yards before opening fire. The execution was frightful. Shayista's elephant was killed under him. As the Moguls staggered back in disorder a party of Maratha cavalry, uttering their wild pæan, dashed upon them.

Shayista Khan, retreating rapidly with his shattered forces, was heard muttering disconnected phrases about treachery and treason. It was evening when he reached Poona and turning back to glare at the hills he saw that on every summit bonfires had been lit by the triumphant Marathas, and as new fuel was piled on them the flames streamed heavenward, illumining the green afterglow of twilight.

Shayista Khan retired to his palace where he remained in seclusion for some days; only emerging to order the evacuation of Poona.[1]

The news of Shivaji's extraordinary exploit caused the utmost consternation in Delhi, where magic powers were attributed to him by the superstitious. An English factor noted that "Report hath made him an Airy Body and added Wings, or else it were impossible for him to be in so many places as

[1] This exploit was imitated by a Maratha captain after Shivaji's death. With two thousand men he fell upon the Imperial camp, and cut his way to Aurangzeb's tent, only to find that the Emperor, in his terror of treachery, never slept in it. He returned with the gold tent-poles as trophies.

he is said to be all at one time. They ascribe to him to perform more than a Herculean labour that he is become the Talk of all conditions of people."

The same astonishment at Shivaji's feats was expressed among the Portuguese in Goa and Senhor da Guarda wrote, "The question is still unsolved whether Sevagy substituted others for himself or he is a Magician or the Devil."[1]

In Court circles there was bitter mortification at the ludicrous failure of the Emperor's uncle and at the jibes which circulated in the Bazar (where Prince Dara's memory was still cherished) at the picture of a Premier Peer losing his thumb and taking refuge among his slave-girls. The Emperor wrote coldly to his uncle, relieving him of his command and transferring him to the governorship of Bengal, an inferior appointment, for that province, though offering almost unlimited opportunities for plunder, was disliked for its unhealthy climate—"the hell well-stocked with bread" it was called. English writers have expended some sympathy on Shayista Khan, but he seems to deserve none. Having made himself a laughing-stock by his conduct of the war in the Deccan, he so dis-

[1] *Vida e accoens do famoso e felicissimo Sevagy*, quoted in Sen's *Military System of the Marathas.* Of these two descents on Poona, the second is related not only by Maratha chroniclers, but also by European contemporaries like Bernier and Manucci. For the first the only evidence is Maratha tradition, and the sceptical may dismiss it as an Angels-of-Mons myth. I have, however, related the story, since every Maratha believes it.

tinguished himself by his rapacity in Bengal that his name is remembered there till this day.[1]

Prince Muazzam, the Emperor's son, succeeded Shayista Khan.

It would have been well for the future of his Empire if Aurangzeb had himself taken command of the army of the south, for he was a competent general, while his son was idle and comfort loving, his chief interest being hunting and polo. But Aurangzeb's favourite sister, the sinister Roshanara, whose intrigues had been of such assistance to him in overcoming Dara, had set her heart on a visit to Kashmir; and Aurangzeb never imagined that the Maratha war, which was to develop into the Spanish ulcer of his Empire, could be of such importance as to make him break his promise to take his sister to the Paradise of the Indies.

Roshanara was perhaps the only person whom Aurangzeb cared for. Far from sharing his Puritan tastes, however, she loved ostentation and luxury. When she appeared in public she rode upon a Burmese elephant hung with enormous bells. The howdah was of gold adorned with amethysts, with carved lattices and a silken net for roof. She was fanned continually by kneeling slave-girls with peacocks' feathers, and on either side of her elephant

[1] It is applied as a term of abuse to unpopular officials, as Nadir Shah is in North-Western India.

rode her eunuchs, fantastically attired, each carrying a silver wand, and a multitude of lackeys with large canes cleared the streets for her passage. She was followed by a procession of her principal ladies-in-waiting, the whole cortège sometimes consisting of sixty elephants of state with attendant outriders. Even the critical Monsieur Bernier was enraptured, and had he not "regarded this display of magnificence with a sort of philosophical indifference, I should have been apt to be carried away by such flights of imagination as inspire most of the *Indian* poets, when they represent the elephants as conveying so many goddesses concealed from the vulgar gaze."

Monsieur Bernier accompanied the Emperor on this visit to Kashmir,[1] and while complaining of the heat and discomfort and slow pace of the expedition, he was impressed by the military pomp of the Imperial camp; the Emperor's tent of scarlet cloth, lined inside with brocade, with hand-painted silk, and with "rich figured satin of various colours and embroideries, silver and gold, with deep and elegant fringes"; the standard bearers, chosen for their beauty, who by day surrounded the tent, holding aloft the insignia of Mogul royalty, the two silver

[1] He was anxious to ascertain whether the inhabitants of Kashmir were really Jews, and was impressed by the frequency of the names Musa and Solomon in that country. There had been Jewish traders in Kashmir since the tenth century as noted by Alberuni (English trans. E. C. Sachan) in his account of his visit to Kashmir. But, of course, the Kashmiris are not really Jews, in spite of even modern theories on this topic.

Fishes, the two Dragons, the gold scales, the open Hands raised in arrogant command, and the personal standard of the Emperor, a couchant lion casting a shadow over the sun; the nobles, who at twilight proceeded in solemn state to pay obeisance to the Emperor—"a grand and imposing spectacle on a dark night to behold, long rows of torches lighting these *Nobles* through extended lines of tents and attending them back again" to their own tents, which were "lined with *Masulipatam* chintz, painted over with flowers of a hundred different kinds."

The natural slowness of an oriental journey was increased by the grand hunting expeditions in which Aurangzeb, like all his dynasty, indulged. But his puritan nature made him attribute his addiction to field sports to reasons other than mere pleasure. His chronicler primly explains: "His Majesty makes hunting a means of increasing his knowledge; and, besides, he uses hunting parties as occasions to inquire into the conditions of the people. On account of such higher motives, His Majesty indulges in the chase. Short-sighted observers think that His Majesty has no other object in view but hunting; but the wise and experienced know that he pursues nobler aims."

CHAPTER TWELVE

WHILE the cortège of the Emperor moved forward by slow stages towards Kashmir, and Prince Muazzam dawdled about in Central India giving parties and playing polo, Shivaji, in revenge for the occupation of Poona, prepared a counter-thrust against one of the trade arteries of the Empire.

The richest emporium in India at this time was Surat. From here the great pilgrim fleets set out yearly for Mecca, and hither came Arab dhows and Chinese junks, French, English, Dutch and Portuguese merchantmen, carrying European and African commodities and bringing traders of all races to traffic in the bazars. So rich was the merchandise pouring into Surat that the customs revenue of this town alone amounted to over seventy thousand pounds annually in the coinage of that day. Surat is on the River Tapti. The currents run swiftly and the tides vary considerably. In Shivaji's time, at the spring tides ships of 1000 tons anchored beside the city itself; but ordinarily only fifty-ton coasting vessels ran so far up the river. Generally all the merchantmen anchored at Swally, the port of Surat. Here it was common to see more than a hundred foreign vessels riding at anchor, English and Dutch being the most numerous, and Arab vessels conspicuous with their enormous streamers of blood-red silk. At the quay were the stores and godowns of the foreign merchants, the roofs of each building displaying some or other national emblem or colour. On arrival at this gateway of the Empire each traveller and merchant had to pass through the Customs House, even to reach which required a long argument and endless bargaining with the porters. The chief customs officer superintended the examination of the luggage and merchandise. He was attended by negro slaves with whips. The examination was severe. Every package had to be opened. The French traveller, Thevenot, even complained that, "Il faut oter le bonnet, la ceinture, les souliers, les chaussures et le reste des habits." After the Customs House one had to pass through the Exchange Office, where foreign currency was changed and where, if one had a credit with an Indian bank, one presented one's *hundis.*[1] Then the traveller set out for Surat in one of the two-wheeled chariots that plied for hire outside the Exchange office—or, if he were a foreigner of consequence, he travelled in a ponderous bullock cart, upholstered in silk. The road was pleasant, shaded with trees and bordered with fields of sugar

[1] This form of the cheque system has been in operation in India since times immemorial, and is still the ordinary means of currency and credit operation.

cane and tobacco, and as he approached the city the traveller would notice with pleasure the numerous gardens which, "shaded from the beams of the sun and refreshed by the neighbourhood of Tanks and Waterworks," were the resort of rich merchants who came there to picnic on holidays. Even the grave English could condescend to visit them, driving "in large coaches, all open, except their wives are in them; the several knobs about them are all covered with silver, and they are drawn by a pair of stately oxen."[1] Besides these public parks every well-to-do merchant prided himself on his private garden outside the walls where they would "feast in pleasant Choultries or Summer-Houses, spread after the Moors' manner with Carpets, refreshed with various Figures of Rising Water out of several Spouts from square Tanks Pargetted." [2] Passing into the City, the visitor would be struck by the "many noble lofty Houses of the Moor Merchants, flat at top, and Terassed with Plaster." But the visitor, if a European, would remark that very few of these buildings had glass windows. Glass was not manufactured locally, and had to be imported from Venice or Constantinople; so the windows were generally "skreened with Cheeks or Latises, carved in wood or Ising-glass, or more commonly Oister-shells." In these palaces the merchant princes lived leisurely lives, and "as they

[1] Ovington. [2] Fryer.

are Neat in Apparel, they are Grave in their Carriage."[1]

The administration of the City was presided over by a Governor, a deputy-Governor, a Judge and a Chief of Police. Every morning the Governor went in procession through the town to the Hall of Justice accompanied by three hundred footguards, three war-elephants decked with cloth of gold, forty horseguards and twenty-four banners of State. There followed him the Judge with a retinue as large. They were attended by "Loud Trumpetts, made as big and like Stentoro Phonica or Speaking Trumpets with thundering kettle-drums." The Chief of Police was little in evidence during the day, but at night "he is heard by his Drums and Trumpets, shouting and hallooing to his Crew in their Perambulation of the City with Lights and Flambeaus."[2]

The foreign merchants found it useful to imitate the pomp of local officials; and the president of the English company always appeared in public with the same state as a noble of the Imperial Court. Preceded by a white Horse of State, by trumpeters and macebearers, and by a "Flag-man carrying St. George, his Colours Swallow-tailed in Silk, fastened to a Silver Partisan," he reclined in a palanquin while servants fanned him with ostrich feathers. His factory was the richest in Surat, trading in

[1] Fryer. [2] *Idem.*

sugar, tea, porcelain and copper from China (carried chiefly in Arab bottoms, the dhow having gradually ousted the junk from Indian waters), cowries from Siam, and gold and ivory from Sumatra. Perhaps, of all those commodities, the English valued their tea most; for, according to Ovington, it was their favourite medicine for curing "headache, gravel, griping in the guts, gout, stone, agues, rheumatisms and catarrhs." The Dutch traded chiefly in jewellery and in spices from Batavia. The French factory was of less importance, being "better stor'd with Monsieurs than with Cash."

Akbar had caused the city to be fortified a century before, and the Governor was allotted a yearly sum sufficient for the upkeep of the garrison. Unfortunately for the Empire and for the citizens of Surat, the present governor was as corrupt as he was cowardly. He arranged for the transfer of most of the garrison on various pretexts in order to embezzle their pay. In other trading cities of the East the richer merchants were accustomed to hire private guards for their mansions and warehouses; but in Surat this custom had fallen into disuse, so general was the sense of security, so great the confidence in Imperial protection.

In December, 1663, a beggar, very ragged and dirty, having no possessions but a bamboo staff and begging bowl, limped along the coast road to

Surat.[1] Indian roads were as crowded then with mendicants as they are now, and this particular beggar excited no comment. If he stopped for a while in some bazar, squatting humbly on the outskirts of a group engaged in conversation, no one troubled to notice (for Indian beggars are notoriously inquisitive) how eagerly he listened when people gossiped of politics in Surat, of the increasing corruption and inefficiency of the administration, or of the doings of that devil Shivaji. It was known that Shivaji was planning an attack on the Portuguese dominions, for (as the gossips reminded each other) every traveller spoke of the large Maratha army menacing the Portuguese town of Bassein as though awaiting a favourable occasion for assault. . . . And had not Shivaji been heard to boast openly that he would shortly attack Goa and loot its golden churches? All the café politicians in Western India were amused at this new example of Shivaji's reckless aggression; not satisfied with a war with the Empire, he now wanted to provoke the Portuguese to hostilities. Only the English agent at Surat was suspicious of this loudly advertised attack on Portuguese territory. "That he (Shivaji) will lay siege to Goa," wrote this sensible business man, "we do hardly believe, in regard it is none of his business to lay siege to any place that is so fortified against him. He is, and

[1] Thevenot.

ever was, for a Running Banquet." But no one else seems to have been equally shrewd, and the beggar must have smiled to find how general was the belief in Shivaji's imminent assault on the Portuguese.

So the beggar returned down the coast road again and disappeared the same day that Shivaji reappeared in his camp. A few nights later, with four thousand cavalry, Shivaji stole out of the camp. It was a dark night. So secret was Shivaji's departure that none of his own officers knew of it—only the men whom he himself had chosen and sworn to secrecy. Riding with great speed, he traversed Imperial territory without opposition and arrived within sight of Surat a few days after his disappearance from his camp had been noted.

On Tuesday, January 5th, 1664, the citizens of Surat awoke to the news that Shivaji was encamped ten miles from the City. There were no troops to resist him, only a few guardsmen in gaudy uniforms accustomed more to the ceremonies of the Governor's court rather than to serious fighting. The main Mogul army, engaged in what they imagined were operations against the Maratha forces, was scattered over a hundred miles away to the south-east.

The Governor sent an envoy to treat with Shivaji, but when he learnt that the Marathas had sent back the envoy, had struck camp and were advancing on the town, the Governor lost his head, and shut himself up in the citadel with his guardsmen and lackeys, leaving the town to the mercy of the Marathas. As Shivaji approached, panic reigned in the quarters of the rich. Futile attempts were made to bury or conceal the accumulated wealth of years. The poor, carrying their possessions with them, scrambled into fishing-boats and canoes to escape downstream, or scattered over the countryside, hiding in the woods and hedgerows.

Now Shivaji had arrived at the walls of Surat. He halted his troops and sent an ultimatum to the Governor, offering to spare the city if its three richest Muhammadan merchants presented themselves at his camp to ransom themselves and their fellow-citizens. A reasonable proposal; but the Governor seems to have been too alarmed even to consider it; or perhaps he consoled himself with the reflection that whatever happened to the city he himself was safe behind his citadel walls. No reply being received to his offer, and the gates being forced without difficulty, Shivaji, a drawn sword in his hand, entered Surat at noon on Wednesday the sixth.

In the absence of either formal submission or surrender by the Civil authorities, Shivaji gave permission to his troops to sack the almost deserted city. The only resistance encountered was from the Dutch and English merchants, who shut themselves up in their factories and refused to admit the Marathas. The English in particular "performed wonders, and saved not only their own houses but those of their neighbours."[1] They even went to the assistance of a rich Muhammadan merchant, Said Beg, one of the three whose attendance at his camp Shivaji had required to ransom the city. They stationed musketeers round his house, and when some Marathas appeared, opened fire. Shivaji at once sent a message to the English, ordering them not to obstruct his troops. But the President of the Company, Sir George Oxindon, considering that it was "more like Englishmen to make ourselves ready to defend our lives and goods," drew up his handful of men "in rank and file with Drum and Trumpet," and replied defiantly to Shivaji, "We are ready for you, and resolved not to go away."

The courage of the English President was widely commended. "He defended himself and his Merchants so bravely, that he had a *Collat* or *Serpaw*, a Robe of Honour from Head to Foot, offered him from the *Great Mogul*, with an abatement of Customs to two-and-a-half *per cent.* granted to the Company, for which his Masters, as a token of the high sense they had of his Valour, presented him with a Medal of Gold with this Device: *Non mina est virtus quam quærere parta tueri.*"[2]

Shivaji himself was impressed by the resolute

[1] Bernier [2] Fryer.

bearing of these foreign traders, and his men made no further move against them. But the plight of the native merchants, who had neither fled nor were lucky enough to have such staunch friends, was pitiable. There were, however, many instances of Shivaji's usual humanity. The houses and property of all Christian priests and missionaries were protected from harm. "The *Frankish* padrys," announced Shivaji to his troops, "are good men. They shall not be molested." [1] A French Capuchin missionary presented himself before Shivaji to beg that his converts and mission servants should not be harmed. Shivaji received him with great kindness, and issued another proclamation ordering that even the houses of Father Ambrose's flock should be exempt from the sack. Moreover, when Shivaji heard that a certain rich trader had been charitable to the Christian missionaries and had supplied them throughout the year with gifts of rice, butter and vegetables, he ordered that neither the man nor his property should be touched, and dispatched soldiers to guard his house from harm.

Nevertheless the sack was extremely thorough. From Wednesday to Saturday the houses, factories and shops were looted systematically and methodically. Many of the houses caught fire, probably on account of the random exchange of shots between the bands of marauding Marathas and the Gover-

[1] Bernier.

nor's soldiers in the citadel. Indeed it is probable that the fort artillery, which opened fire in sudden bursts of futile activity without inflicting any damage on the invaders, caused more destruction of property than the calculated devastations of the Marathas. By Friday two-thirds of the town had been destroyed by fire, and the English Chaplain recorded that "the fire turned night into day, as before the smoke in the daytime had turned day into night, rising so thick that it darkened the Sun like a great cloud."

Many Imperialist soldiers who had been left behind in the Governor's scamper to the fort were taken prisoner, and on Thursday evening an ugly incident nearly turned the sack into a massacre. The Mogul Governor, after brooding for two days nervously behind the walls of the fort, sent out a young officer to assassinate Shivaji. He pretended to be an envoy from the Governor offering to arrange for the surrender of the fort. This was not of great interest to Shivaji, for he never meant to hold the city, and did not intend to risk the lives of his men either in attacking or retaining the citadel. But when the young officer begged for an interview Shivaji agreed to see him. When he was shown into Shivaji's tent, Shivaji (perhaps remembering how Shayista Khan had taunted him with cowardice) greeted the Governor's envoy with similar heavy pleasantries. "Your master," he said, "sits timidly at home like a shy girl." The young Muhammadan, who evidently had little liking for his present mission, muttered angrily: "We are not all girls." But when Shivaji continued to banter him he lost his temper and ran at Shivaji with a dagger. A Maratha guardsman sprang forward and slashed off the Muhammadan's hand, but so great was the force of his attack that he bore Shivaji down, and the two rolled together on the ground. The guardsman, standing over them, hacked at the Muhammadan's turbanned helmet and cut through his skull.

But a rumour had flashed round the Maratha camp that Shivaji had been assassinated. There rose a bitter cry for vengeance, wild voices shouting for mass-executions in reprisal. Shivaji, his dress still splashed with blood, staggered to his feet and ran through the camp, showing himself to his followers, ordering them back to their duties. But even his magic voice for once almost failed of its effect. It was only when he agreed to exact some retribution from his prisoners that the soldiers' fury was assuaged. Then Shivaji ordered four of his Imperialist prisoners to be beheaded and the hands of twenty-four others to be cut off. It is worth recording that one of the prisoners led out to execution was an Englishman who had been captured along with several Mogul soldiers. When he took off his hat and his complexion proclaimed his nationality,

Shivaji (in spite of the irritation he could be excused for feeling against those defiant, interfering foreign traders) at once released him and sent him under escort to the English factory. In spite of this instance of clemency, the penalty exacted from innocent men for a single act of treachery will seem to modern readers, accustomed to the more scientific methods of reprisal employed in Western warfare, needlessly cruel; but it should be remembered that probably only some such signal, even melodramatic, act of reprisal would have avoided a savage outbreak by the wilder elements of the Maratha force, which during its march north had been joined by motley bands of Hindu tribesmen anxious to follow the standards of the Liberator.

Early on Sunday morning news came that a Mogul army was advancing to the relief of the city. The Marathas had already collected their booty. It was enormous. "Millions in money and goods," complained Khafi Khan, "came into the hands of that evil infidel Shivaji." The Marathas loaded their horses with "the stuffs of Kashmir and Ahmedabad," and with "gold, silver, pearls, diamonds and such precious ware," and evading the approaching Mogul army, rode with their usual speed down the coast to Raigad, Shivaji's capital.

Not till the vanguard of the Imperialist army entered Surat did the Governor venture out of the citadel. When he did, he was greeted with shouts of abuse, with curses and hisses. His son, braver against unarmed traders than against Marathas, raised his gun and shot one of the demonstrators dead. Thereupon a deputation of citizens waited on the General of the newly-arrived army, clamouring against the Governor and praising the bravery of the English whose conduct during the sack had formed so remarkable a contrast to that of the Imperial officials. They begged that the English President should be given some reward.

The General called on Sir George Oxindon and offered him a gold vest, a horse and a sword. But Oxindon, more modest and fastidious than the Nabobs and conquistadors of the following century, declined these gifts, remarking that "they were becoming to a Soldier, but we were Merchants."

CHAPTER THIRTEEN

THE Emperor was deeply mortified by the news from Surat. Dervishes and priests publicly lamented that so orthodox an Emperor had allowed that great city—so frequented by the devout bound for the birthplace of the Prophet, the city known as the Door of Pious Pilgrimage and the Gateway of Mecca—be entered with ease and looted at leisure by a Kaffir. The palace women set up a great lamentation led by Shayista Khan's wife (who had not followed her husband to Bengal, but had remained behind at Court—where she was intimate with Princess Roshanara—in order to inflame the anger of the Emperor against the Hindu rebel who had killed her son and inflicted so humiliating a revenge on her husband). While the Emperor brooded morosely alone in his chamber, messengers brought him intelligence of further misfortunes. His son, Prince Muazzam, who had failed either to save Surat or to intercept Shivaji doing his retreat, now, stung by his father's reproaches, advanced clumsily into Maratha territory, and was repulsed in an assault on Sinhgad. He had no enthusiasm for war and no plan of campaign, and when not hunting or playing polo he would grumble to his friends about the discomforts of military life.

After his repulse he attempted no further advance, but hovered uncertainly along the frontier marches till the monsoon broke and immobilised his army with its artillery and cumbrous baggage train. But the rain was no obstacle to Shivaji's light cavalry, and all that monsoon of 1664 he devastated Imperial territory, swerving past the Mogul lines and swooping upon town after town. "Shivaji and his scouts," reported the English, "range all over the country, making Havoc wherever he comes with Fire and Sword."

The Moguls seemed, for the moment, helpless against an enemy who "seemed to be everywhere and prepared for every emergency." No calculation of his movements seemed possible, all provision against attack futile, so sudden were his lightning strokes. Garrisons were strengthened, only to be isolated from the main army by enveloping raids, reinforcements hurried up to remote outposts only to find a smoking ruin and a few abandoned guns.

"He is," wrote an English factor, "very nimble and active, imposing strange labour on himself that he may endure hardship, and also exercises his chiefest men that he flies to and fro with incredible dexterity." There has never been so skilful a guerrilla leader as Shivaji, and the Moguls were bewildered by his tactics. So far from occupying Maratha territory, they found themselves unable to protect Imperial territory from invasion and pillage, with the result that the whole country fell into "a confused condition."

Several of the Muhammadan barons owning allegiance to Bijapur profited by the confusion to follow in Shivaji's wake and loot the districts that the Marathas conquered. Of one of these, Rustam by name, the English factors wrote: "He hath begun to taste the sweetness of plunder, so that in a short time he will get a habit of it."

Shivaji, unlike the Imperial authorities, had realised the value of sea-power and the strength it gave to the foreigners settled in the western ports. He had begun to build a navy, as a further weapon against the Empire.

It was not difficult to recruit sailors. Along the coast, in villages of heavily-thatched, squat cottages, surrounded by groves of palm and coconut, the thin, silver-brown trunks all leaning landward, fisherfolk of certain Hindu clans racially allied to the Marathas had from early days developed considerable skill in seamanship. Their vessels were rude craft more remarkable for the pretty carvings on their prows than for any qualities of construction, but the men who sailed in them were afraid neither of storm nor of Arab warships, and knew the ways of all the tides and currents and every mile of the almost endless inlets and creeks with which that coast is seamed. Organised into the nucleus of a navy, they became a terror to Mogul traders.

The pilgrimage to Mecca became a perilous enterprise, and as long as they were in Indian waters anxious merchants leaning along the bulwarks of every Mogul ship scanned the horizon for sign of a low, narrow hulk and a great triangular sail of flaming ochre.

And in the track of naval aggression went trading enterprise. Already in 1663 Shivaji had sent two merchantment to Arabia; and two years later the English reported that he was sending out two trading vessels a year from each of his "nine most considerable ports" to Persia, Irak and Arabia. And Shivaji, with his usual foresight, understood the value of sea communications on a campaign, and used his ships to increase the mobility of his army. For the first time, in February, 1665, he transported the whole of his effective army in eighty-five frigates and three large merchantmen down the coast to deliver a surprise attack.

Nevertheless, in spite of Shivaji's interest in his navy, he was a true hillman, without instinct or tradition in naval matters, and his ships were, by contemporary European standard, of poor quality. Though a terror to European trading vessels, they were greatly inferior to European warships. An English official dismissed them as "pitiful things, so that one good English ship would destroy a hundred of them without running herself into great danger." They were mostly "vessels of shallow burden capable of taking close refuge under every shelter of the land . . . and they trusted to the superiority of number (and not of gun-power or seaworthiness) against ships in the open sea." [1]

The only considerable engagement between Maratha and English ships took place on 18th October, 1679. A Maratha officer named Mai Nayah landed some 150 men on the island of Khanderi, near Bombay. This caused great alarm to the English, who ordered them to "quit that place," otherwise they would "repel them with force as an open and public enemy." The Marathas declined, and English and Maratha ships came into collision. Though an oddly inconclusive affair, the battle proved, in fact, a reverse for the Marathas, in spite of the fact that they had sixty small vessels against eight. Before the actual engagement the English lost a ship owing to the misconduct of "a Lieutenant who in a fit of drunkenness landed with the men of his shibar, was killed with six other Europeans, the rest made prisoners and the shibar hauled up on the shore." [2] During the seafight it seemed at first that the Marathas' great speed and skill in manœuvring would more than compensate for the English superiority in

[1] Orme, who adds that Shivaji "wished to command his fleet in person and tried the element; but his constitution could not overcome the nausea."
[2] Orme.

guns; and within half an hour an English ship, the *Dover*, commanded by one Sergeant Mauleverer. struck her colours and was boarded by the Marathas, Five of the remaining English vessels retreated hastily towards Bombay, but a powerful sixteen-gun frigate, appropriately named the *Revenge*, remained to oppose the whole Maratha fleet and sank five enemy ships without suffering damage. The Marathas then drew off, leaving the *Revenge* triumphant. The Surat Council was annoyed that the victory had not been more conclusive, and were severe on Sergeant Mauleverer and his men, and wrote, "We, having duly considered, and perceiving how cowardly they behaved themselves in the time of engagement, do order them to be stricken out of the muster roles, but, that they may not wholly perish, that some small allowance be made to them for victuals."

In spite of this naval encounter, the English were unable to eject the Marathas from Khanderi. They contrived, as the Surat Council complained, "to fortify and store the island maugre all our designs." If he could not bring pressure on Bombay by sea, Shivaji could threaten the English by land, and he sent four thousand men to the borders of English territory. The Surat Council then decided that it would be better "honourably to withdraw themselves in time," and wrote a querulous letter to Shivaji, complaining that his menacing gesture was "not in the least becoming in a Prince of his Eminence and qualifications, yet to show the Candour of our Proceedings, we are willing to forget the past," and so, in spite of English superiority at sea, Khanderi Island remained in Maratha hands.[1]

Nor was it only the English who proved more than a match for the Marathas at sea. The Abyssinian pirates of Janjira Island resisted all Maratha attempts on their stronghold. With wearisome regularity Shivaji organised attacks on Janjira and Danda-Rajpuri, "resolved to take that Castle, let it cost him what it will"; constructed floating batteries; tried to throw a mole across the sea from the mainland to Janjira Island; intrigued with the English for the loan of their superior naval artillery and was met with evasive replies from the English President, who had decided "not to positively promise him grenadoes nor to absolutely deny him." But each expedition ended in failure, and always, as the Maratha chronicler sadly noted, "the Maharaja's men returned disappointed." In fact, the State of Janjira[2] survives to this day, ruled by the descendants of the pirate Chieftains against whom Shivaji struggled.

By the end of the monsoon of 1664 the question

[1] It should be remembered that incidents such as a single sea-fight did not mean actual war any more than struggles between English and French colonists in America in the following century necessarily involved their respective governments in hostilities.

[2] Janjira is a Marathi corruption of the Arabic word *jazira*, meaning an island, which these Abyssinians used to describe their rocky fastness.

of Shivaji absorbed the attention of the Imperial government to the exclusion of almost all other interests. Aurangzeb could hardly refer to, or bear mention of, the "Mountain Rat," as he contemptuously named the Maratha leader, without a bitter outburst against the incompetence of his son and the ineptitude of his officers. Finally, on his birthday, September 30th, he convened a Durbar, and after receiving the congratulations of his courtiers, ordered the herald to proclaim the list of Birthday Honours. The first of these was the appointment, in succession to Prince Muazzam, of Raja Jai Sing, to the command of the Army of the South in action against the Marathas.

It must have been infinitely disagreeable to the Imperial bigot to admit the successive failures of both his uncle and son and to elevate to the office they had disgraced a Hindu general.

But Jai Sing was an admirable choice. He was a cadet of the great House of Jaipur, of which the present Maharaja is the thirty-seventh Prince in direct succession. An orphan at the age of twelve, he had enlisted in the Mogul army and seen his first action as a child. By slow stages he had risen, commended by successive superiors for his extraordinary bravery, the traditionally desperate and fatalistic courage of a Rajput knight—the courage that to a Rajput is the only manly virtue. Like every Rajput, he had been brought up on the ballads of his kingdom, that tell of the old heroes of militant Hinduism whose lives were but the preparation for death (for as in the lay of the Vikings defeat, not success, is the endearing quality of the hero), whether in battle against the Muslim or in a duel fought upon some trifling point of honour, in perils lightly run in obedience to his lady or for the defence of his master—terrible deaths of torture, when the hero smiled and fell asleep under the instruments of his tormentors, or deaths of spectacular melodrama, as when a prince, a commander of a besieging army, rather than expose his elephant to the hedge of spikes in the gate of the invested town, dashed his own brains out upon a spike-point, thus offering his own body as a shield for the assailants against the spikes. Inspired by such traditions, Jai Sing had proved himself as wildly brave as any of his ancestors. Now, at the age of sixty, the greatest of all the feudatory nobles, he ranked immediately after the Princes of the Blood. The reckless cavalier had grown into a shrewd and cautious commander, a wise counsellor and skilful diplomat, employing four languages with equal ease. With the name and prestige of a princely family, he brought to the parvenu Mogul court the subtlety and exquisite address of an ancient culture.

It was on the allegiance of the Rajput clans that Akbar had based the stability of his empire. Rajput nobles were tempted to court and appointed to high office, Rajput princesses were accepted in marriage by the Emperors. Rajput dress was copied and the Rajput style and idiom sensibly affected the art of the Imperial capital. But the Rajputs had never accepted as inevitable the Mogul domination. And Jai Sing, with his Rajput's age-old traditions of an almost endless crusade against Islam, accepted the command against a Hindu leader with a heavy heart; perhaps only his soldier's oath of allegiance to the Emperor overcame his hesitation. The Emperor had assured him in phrases as cordial as they were rare in Aurangzeb's mouth that only he could restore the military situation on the southern frontier. He had risen from the Peacock Throne and placed round Jai Sing's neck his own pearl necklace. Yet, like so many Rajputs of that time, Jai Sing felt increasingly uneasy at the position of Hindus in the Empire; the tolerance of former reigns had given place to hardening discrimination. Jai Sing must have felt like a pagan general in the days of Theodosius, serving without enthusiasm in his old age under the lengthening shadow of the Labarum, but tied by a lifetime of memories and associations to the profession of arms.

Sighing heavily, he climbed into his palanquin and, surrounded by the horsemen of his escort, who awaited him outside the great gate of the Palace, he was borne off to his house.

CHAPTER FOURTEEN

BEFORE proceeding south, Jai Sing demanded from the Emperor complete power both civil and military in the districts under his control. If he was to finish the campaign quickly he wanted no "advisers" from Delhi, no instructions from officious cabinet ministers, no allocation of conquered territory to courtiers of royal relatives. No Mogul general had been given such authority before. But Aurangzeb (who remembered the circumstances of his own accession to the throne and would have hesitated to entrust such power to a Mogul noble, still less to a son or cousin) had no suspicions of Jai Sing's motives, and he consented. Nevertheless, he could not resist pestering Jai Sing throughout the campaigns with suggestions and instructions which, like those of Napoleon dispatched from Dresden or Smolensk to his generals in Spain, were always months out of date by the time they arrived. But Jai Sing ignored the Imperial essays in strategy, or, when an answer was peremptorily demanded, replied soothingly but vaguely that he was "busy about the task on which I have been sent."

Jai Sing settled down quietly to his preparations.

He collected as reinforcements for the Army of the South fourteen thousand cavalry, many of them his own Rajput clansmen, and a strong contingent of Afghan infantry under a capable but violent Afghan, Dilir Khan. This officer was famous as "a great eater and very strong, and in drawing the bow none could vie with him. Once he was passing through the great North Gate of Delhi when he laid hold of one of the elephant spikes of the gate and twisted it round with one hand. 'You can still see it in that condition, it having been left thus in memory of him.'"[1]

As his chief officer of artillery Jai Sing chose the Italian adventurer Manucci, who had been a great favourite of his ever since he taught him how to play the card-game, Hombre. They used to sit up night after night, and Manucci won large sums from Jai Sing. Except as an amusing companion, Manucci would not seem as yet to have showed any qualities justifying Jai Sing's offer of so responsible a position—but the appointment, as it turned out, was an admirable one. Manucci chose three other Europeans as his subordinates, a Frenchman, an Englishman and a Portuguese. They not only organised Jai Sing's train of artillery, but began to train the Rajput cavalry to charge in European fashion, discharging pistols as they rode at the enemy, while Jai Sing watched their manœuvres approvingly from the

[1] Irvine's *Storia do Mogor*, quoting O.D. 45 *Réserve.*

back of his elephant and talked of sending to Europe to hire a whole regiment of European horsemen.

Manucci intrigued the other Imperialist officers by wearing his gown fastened on the right in Musulman fashion (Hindus button their coats on the left), but wearing his moustache like a Rajput, so they asked him, since his appearance was half Hindu, half Muslim, what religion he really followed. When Manucci said portentously, "I am Christian," they answered testily, "Yes, yes. But a Hindu Christian or a Muhammadan Christian?"

By the beginning of 1665 his organisation was complete. Deliberate in preparation, he was rapid in action. He marched south with a speed that would have done credit to Shivaji. Without a day's halt the army—artillerymen, infantry and cavalry—pushed on over the plains that were already tawny with heat-ravaged grass and drooping trees, the sun-scorched soil burning the men's feet and sending up clouds of dust to choke them. Insensible to fatigue, the old Rajput, his brown hand upon his sword-hilt, the caste-mark always freshly painted on his broad forehead, urged on his troops. He reached the headquarters of Prince Muazzam a month after leaving Delhi, distributed his reinforcements among the depleted and discouraged regiments of the southern army and, ordering an immediate advance into Maratha territory, entered Poona a month later.

Now for the first and last time Shivaji was faced with a commander whose military abilities were in the same class as his own. There was a pause as the two antagonists surveyed each other and considered plans of campaign. The hot weather had begun in earnest, and in Poona the narrow streets and close-built houses increased the invaders' discomfort. By day a hot sand-laden wind blew monotonously and at night sleep was difficult in the oppressive stillness. But, undeterred by climate or cramped quarters, the eye-flies at noon or the mosquitoes moaning about his lamp at night, Jai Sing worked indefatigably, studying, reflecting, planning.

His first task was to envelop the territories effectively under Shivaji's control, if not with Mogul lines, at least with forces allied to the Empire. He incited Bijapur to attack Shivaji in the rear and regain its lost territories; in particular he appealed to the son of Afzul Khan, offering him the chance to avenge his father's death, and the lad, eagerly agreeing, arrived at the Mogul camp with a number of retainers. He sent emissaries to all the factories of European traders in the Western ports, pointing out that the rise of Maratha sea-power was a menace to their commerce, and urging them to co-operate with the Empire in exterminating the new kingdom. He sent Manucci to bribe the petty chiefs of the coast jungles to raid Shivaji's outposts.

Manucci proved himself an expert diplomat. He arrived at the court of the Raja of Ramnagar, "whose territories lie amidst frightful hills and gloomy forests," and terrified him with a highly-coloured picture of Mogul vengeance, and excited him with promises of huge rewards. The Rajah, though he finally agreed to co-operate with the Moguls, asked for a few days' delay while he consulted the neighbouring jungle chiefs; and Manucci was glad of a week's idleness, during which he shot and fished. It was very hot weather, and the great brown leaves of the teak-trees stood out straight as though carved out of wood and the red dust-laden air quivered in the endless afternoon, while golden orioles called and birds of paradise flashed like silver fire through the shadows. These lonely ravines were haunts of sorcery and magic. A jungle princeling, who coveted Manucci's horse, given him by Jai Sing, put a spell upon the animal so that it could not move at all, but stood still and lifeless as a statue. Only when Manucci agreed to sell it for three thousand rupees did the horse come to life again. One of Manucci's servants was passing through a field of radishes. He stretched out his hand to pluck a radish and found that he could neither move the radish nor withdraw his hand. There he stayed in a ridiculous cramped posture, bent over the radish, till Manucci arrived, sought out the owner of the field and bribed him to release his servant. The man came and whispered a few words over the radish, and at once Manucci's servant found that his hand was free again.

Finally, by a lavish distribution of gold, Jai Sing's agents tried to corrupt Shivaji's own officers. In this last field of activity Jai Sing's plans proved unfruitful, for only two of Shivaji's officers listened to the overtures of the Mogul agents—and these were not Marathas.

After three weeks of diplomacy, Jai Sing turned his attention to military operations. He was the only Imperialist commander who realised the full importance of that bridge of forts which, it will be remembered, formed the nucleus of Shivaji's power and joined together his territories to west and to east of the western Ghats. If these forts passed into enemy hands, then the Maratha armies would be driven into the open plains, where they could be overwhelmed by superior numbers. Other Imperialist commanders shrank from any such conclusion because of the difficulty of attacking a series of fortresses already famous for their skilfully constructed defences, manned by desperate men and situated in mountainous country, peopled only by wild tribesmen hostile to the invader. Nor in India of that date, though the art of military fortification was as advanced as in Europe, was there any grasp of the methods of siege-operations. Even the great Akbar was often baffled by the resistance of a single fort. In the case of a general delegated by the Emperor to conduct a war there was the added fear of censure, even of disgrace, if a siege lasted too long, the fear, too, of intriguing courtiers whispering suspicions of one's tenderness to the enemy; and there was the greater attraction of strategic gambits and of engagements which could be magnified in dispatches into resounding triumphs. But whereas in other Indian wars, after a victory the enemy forts would probably fall like the branches of a dead tree, with the Marathas the network of mountain forts formed the backbone of the whole body military, and successful actions against the armies in the field were only flesh wounds which, however severe, would not prove fatal. Again, while most Indian armies were composed of the feudal levies of great lords of various race and religion, whose only link was a common, though often remote, allegiance to the sovereign, the Maratha army was a compact force, united in personal devotion to one man, with no divided loyalties between intermediate chiefs, animated by religious enthusiasm and by a real national sense. Yet these very qualities tied the Maratha army, when on the defensive, to its national territory, which was, after all, only a small province which could be easily overrun by superior forces once the back of the resistance was broken. And Jai Sing realised that the focal point of this resistance lay in the chain of mountain forts. He therefore grimly set himself to the task of reducing the fortresses one by one, ignoring all offers of battle, all chances of spectacular victory.

The first place he selected for assault was Purandar, the fort which Shivaji had taken from the three quarrelsome brothers. It is a fortified mountain to the south-west of Poona, rising from the plain in a series of basalt cliffs. It is over four thousand feet high, and on cloudy days its dark crest is hidden. At the summit are two peaks, on one of which is the citadel proper. The other peak, known as Shiva's Rosary, had also been fortified and garrisoned by Shivaji so as to form an outwork of the main fort; a spur of it commanded the western corner of the citadel, and thus made its retention by the defending garrison vital.

Jai Sing threw out blockhouses to bar the approaches to Purandar. Then, towards the end of March, leaving a garrison in Poona, he advanced swiftly with his main force to the plateau of Saswad, six miles to the south of Purandar, to prevent the advance of a relieving force. When the fortress was completely invested he ordered Dilir Khan to open the attack with his Afghans.

Purandar was garrisoned with a thousand men under an officer named Murar. The attacking forces, numbered about twenty thousand and was attended by all Jai Sing's European-officered artillery. The Afghans advanced deliberately, pushing forward their trenches and driving back the Maratha sorties till they were under the great cliff crowned with Shiva's Rosary which was Jai Sing's first objective.

Now the great guns were dragged up the steep hillside, the men bent double as they strained at the ropes, gasping and staggering and choking, while the sun beat down on their backs and the dead grass splintered into a fine dust and the Marathas rained down on them arrows and stones and old kettles full of gunpowder. Every day Jai Sing visited the front lines, praising and encouraging his men, and giving rewards to those who had distinguished themselves in action the previous day.

It took the besiegers a week to get their guns in position opposite the front gateway of Shiva's Rosary. Then a concentrated bombardment was opened at short range. At the same time Jai Sing's sappers set to work mining the walls to left and right of the front gateway. The gateway crumbled under the fierce artillery fire, but the Marathas held on behind the pile of debris, repulsing each assault Next, a mine exploded, carrying away a large part of the wall, and through the smoke and dust Dilir Khan launched his Afghans in a furious thrust. The remnant of the garrison fell back to the shelter of their barracks, behind whose walls they steeled themselves for a final resistance.

Meanwhile, however, the commandant of the main fort, realising how difficult it would be to defend his own lines once Shiva's Rosary fell, tried to create a diversion. With five hundred men, half his total force, he swept down the hillside on to the flank of the Afghan regiments streaming up to the assault on the Rosary. So violent was the impact of his attack that the wing of the enemy crumpled up and the Marathas penetrated almost to the besiegers' camp, killing seven hundred men—but themselves losing three hundred. Dilir Khan, directing operations from the back of an elephant, watched with composure the approach of the Marathas. When their commander, Murar, was within range, Dilir Khan took careful aim and shot him dead. The Marathas were discouraged by the loss of their leader; the first exhilaration of their charge died away; presently they fell back towards the fort, warding off with difficulty the attacks of the Afghans, who had recovered from their surprise and were trying to cut off their retreat.

All that night Dilir Khan continued his attack on the barracks of Shiva's Rosary, and in the morning Jai Sing rode up in person with a band of picked Rajputs. The garrison were too tired to stand. Their ammunition was exhausted. Backs to the wall they stood awaiting the enemy's final onslaught. Jai Sing remarked their condition and, advancing alone and unarmed, offered them honourable terms. They shrugged their shoulders. They had no alternative but to accept. They stumbled out into the sunshine, limping from many wounds, their faces black with smoke. Jai Sing received them with true Rajput chivalry. As a fellow-Hindu he congratulated them on their courage. He embraced them one by one—they in their blood-soaked rags and he in his silk and muslin—and invested them with robes of honour. After further compliments he set them free and invited them to return to their homes.

Then he sent a herald to the main fortress offering similar terms. The herald concluded: "Surrender, Marathas! Your commandant is dead."

The Marathas shouted back: "We hope to die as bravely as he did."

So the guns were dragged forward once again and siege operations recommenced.

Meanwhile Shivaji had not been idle. He could not engage in open battle the Mogul army concentrated at Saswad, for any striking force that he could raise would be outnumbered by three or four to one. His only hope was to create diversions that would induce Jai Sing to divide his forces. His activity and energy aroused even his enemies' astonishment. Khafi Khan tells of "assaults by night, captures of outposts and burnings of jungles."

With his navy he raided the Mogul coast, seized ports in Gujarat and fell upon the sea-borne trade of Bijapur in revenge for aid given to the Moguls.

But Jai Sing refused to be drawn. He ignored minor revenges and local losses. He hung on to the siege of Purandar, assuring the Emperor, who was full of anxiety for the effect on his subjects' loyalty of the continual raids on the cities of Gujarat, that his soldiers were "doing here in a day what could not be achieved elsewhere in a month."

When he saw that the fall of Purandar was only a matter of time, Jai Sing left Dilir Khan with sufficient forces to complete his task, and with his main army struck suddenly eastward through the hills, brushing aside the frenzied sallies of the hillmen. He reached Rajgad before Shivaji was aware of his move, and in Rajgad, as Jai Sing had learnt from his spies, were Shivaji's family. He set about the siege of Rajgad with his usual deliberation and care. As soon as the investing trenches were completed and fortified strongly enough to offer reasonable security from any relieving forces, Jai Sing sent out columns to ravage the Maratha villages in the plains with calculated severity. At the same time he treated with the utmost kindness any Marathas who surrendered, hoping by this double policy to break their attachment to Shivaji. Shivaji saw his state crumbling to pieces before his eyes. His efforts to relieve Purandar had all failed, and now Jai Sing's grip was tightening on Rajgad, where he would, if successful, possess himself of Shivaji's family, which he might use as hostages.

Shivaji came to a sudden decision to obtain what terms he could before the military situation deteriorated still further. Historians have debated the reasons for what seems a sudden loss of confidence. But Shivaji was always an opportunist. He realised how formidable an opponent Jai Sing was, but at the same time how fair and honourable a man to deal with. In a long and perhaps increasingly unsuccessful war he did not know how long his men would endure against the enormous resources and constantly renewed man-power of the Empire. Time was on Shivaji's side, if one took the longer view. If the struggle were abandoned now it could be recommenced on some future more favourable occasion. It could be no shame now to admit defeat, since for three years a small new state had engaged the whole Mogul Empire on equal terms and frequently with startling success.

At the beginning of June Shivaji sent a message to Jai Sing, begging for an armistice. Jai Sing refused to accept anything less than unconditional surrender. Shivaji then offered to visit the Imperial camp to discuss his personal surrender. Jai Sing sent him a safe-conduct, swearing in the presence of Shivaji's envoy (and, to lend weight to his oath, holding in his hand a spray of sacred basil) that he would hold himself responsible for Shivaji's safety. A Rajput's promise could not be doubted, and Shivaji, no longer riding his white charger, but carried in a single palanquin, set out for the Imperial camp. Jai Sing had returned with his staff to the lines at the foot of Purandar after organising the investment of Rajgad. When he heard that Shivaji was approaching, he sent a Brahman to ask if he really wanted peace. Shivaji, in his palanquin, nodded. Then Jai Sing sent his senior Rajput noble to welcome Shivaji.

Such was Shivaji's reputation that the Imperialist officers found it difficult to believe that Shivaji was really coming to talk peace. They thought his request must be but the preparation for some hideous new "Stratagem," and even Manucci's companions were filled with increasing anxiety, and when it was announced that Shivaji was nearing the Imperial camp it was impossible to persuade people that he was alone, and the soldiers ran about crying that Shivaji was attacking.

In his tent, the great viceregal tent of scarlet cloth hung with carpets and brocades and furnished rather for a banquet than for war, Jai Sing awaited his visitor with curiosity. Round him stood a dozen picked men of his feudal retinue, Rajputs with hung turbans and divided beards flowing down each side of their cuirasses, each holding aloft a naked sword. As soon as Shivaji entered the tent, a slender weary figure, the Rajput guardsmen closed round him. He had become an almost legendary creature, accused of magic arts, and of superhuman cunning. So Jai Sing was taking no chances. But when Shivaji bowed low to Jai Sing, thanking him for receiving him, Jai Sing rose from his couch and folded Shivaji in his arms.

"You have fought well against the Emperor," he said. "Now you must fight as well for him." And, taking him by the hand, he made him sit on the couch beside him.

Jai Sing's words were certainly sincere. He saw no hope for independent Hindu kingdoms. They would be overwhelmed sooner or later. If the traditional champions of Hinduism—the Rajputs—had fallen before the might of the Empire, what hope was there for a new little state of half-civilised hillmen who had never before been known as warriors? And if a prince of the House of Jaipur was not ashamed to serve the Empire, it was hardly for an obscure Maratha to talk about disgrace and humiliation. He went on to remark that Shivaji's undoubted talents as a soldier would find a far wider field for their exercise in the Imperial service, in which one might command the greatest armies in the world and fight battles in Turkestan or in Burma, than in local skirmishes and ambuscades along a few dozen miles of western jungle. "You can, if you submit," he argued, "retain your ancestral territories and such land as you have conquered from Bijapur. But you must hold them as a feudatory of the Empire. If you are ambitious, you may rise to the highest offices in the service of His Majesty."

Shivaji asked about the terms of his submission. They were hard, but not unreasonable. Shivaji was to pay an agreed indemnity and to hand over the keys of twenty-three of his forts and admit into them Mogul garrisons. At first Shivaji refused to consider this proposal. As he haggled with Jai Sing a sudden clamour was heard.

Shivaji started up.

One of the Rajput guardsmen drew aside a curtain of the tent, and Shivaji saw, rising sheer from the outworks of the camp, the dark outline of Purandar, on which Dilir Khan was at that moment renewing his attack. It was a day of stifling heat, that last thunder-heavy heat that comes before the monsoon, draining all colour from the world, drawing up the life of plants and trees as though in a final exhalation of exhaustion.

Jai Sing and Shivaji, standing side by side, watched besiegers and besieged, silhouetted against a steely sky, struggling like feverish insects. Thinly came their cries in the still air and the ceaseless roar of artillery echoed among the basalt cliffs. A bastion fell in, burying its defenders under a shower of bricks and earth. The Afghans rushed in over the smoking debris. Two towers had been captured, and only the inner citadel remained. Already the guns were being dragged into place to batter down this last stronghold over which still fluttered, smoke-blackened and tattered, the ochre banner of the Marathas.

Shivaji turned to Jai Sing and begged him to stop this useless slaughter.

"Your men will surrender in a minute," Jai Sing said.

"Never—without an order from me," Shivaji answered.

Then Jai Sing offered to send a message to Dilir Khan to stay his assault if Shivaji would order his men to surrender with the honours of war. Shivaji agreed. He sent an officer with a letter to his garrison. But those Marathas, though it was clear they could hardly hold out another day, at first refused to believe that Shivaji had sent any such order, and Shivaji had to confirm his instructions with a second messenger.

Dilir Khan was equally dissatisfied. He felt that he had been robbed, by mere negotiated truce, of the glory of the final spectacular assault he was just then preparing. In his rage he flung his turban on the ground, gnashed his teeth and bit pieces of flesh from his wrist. Next day Jai Sing sent a message to him begging him to receive Shivaji. At first this proposal threw Dilir Khan into fresh paroxysms of fury. But Jai Sing insisted; and finally, sulking and resentful, Dilir Khan agreed to the interview. As soon as he met Shivaji he fell under the spell of his extraordinary charm, to which every one who met him testifies. He presented Shivaji with his sword and two of his favourite horses. Jai Sing, delighted at the cordiality with which this unpromising meeting had concluded, clothed Shivaji with an especial robe of honour and gave him an elephant of state and a jewelled spray for his turban.

That night Shivaji entered Jai Sing's tent and found the old Rajput playing cards with his Italian artillery officer, Manucci. They were introduced, and Shivaji, "seeing me," notes Manucci, "a youth, well favoured of body," complimented the European on his fine appearance, adding that he must be a Rajah in his own country. Manucci was delighted by this remark, and Jai Sing (who must have often been amused by Manucci's vanity) joined in the game of flattery, and assured the Italian that nature had given him a mind and body very different from those of others. This set Manucci boasting about the superior qualities of all Europeans. In Europe, he said, the Kings were far greater than here in India. Shivaji, alas, showed himself lamentably ignorant about the power of European monarchs. The only one he had ever heard of, he remarked, was the King of Portugal. Could there be others? But he must have said this to tease Manucci, because he knew something about both English and Dutch, having had some trouble with them in Surat. However, Manucci was very happy to impress Shivaji with a list of other equally powerful monarchs.

The following morning Purandar surrendered to the Imperialists, and the garrison marched out with the honours of war. Shivaji then agreed to hand over twenty-three of his forts and to write a letter to the Emperor, pleading for his favour. By the same postal messenger Jai Sing sent a secret letter to Aurangzeb, suggesting a cordial reply to Shivaji's letter. Generosity at such a moment would, he urged, turn Shivaji's natural sense of humiliation into grateful loyalty. Such chivalry was not, however, native to Aurangzeb. Frigidly he replied to Shivaji: "Your letter, couched in humble strain, has been received by Us. It is agreeable to note that you crave pardon for your conduct, and that you repent of your past deeds. Our reply is that your behaviour has been so base that it deserves no forgiveness. Nevertheless at Raji Jai Sing's intercession we extend to you a general pardon. . . ." It was hardly the tone to turn a defeated opponent into an enthusiastic supporter. However, Shivaji carried out the terms of his treaty with Jai Sing, admitted Imperial governors into the forts agreed on and accepted office in the Mogul army under Jai Sing.

It is possible that as long as Jai Sing remained Viceroy of Central India and Shivaji's immediate superior, Shivaji would have continued loyal to the Emperor. Unfortunately, Aurangzeb, inevitably suspicious of his servants, began to brood over the obvious esteem in which Jai Sing held the former rebel. Two Hindus together—it was natural that even a Rajput, however loyal to his sovereign, would nevertheless be unduly lenient to a co-religionist. Jai Sing had been sent to crush Shivaji and stamp out all semblance of Maratha independence; instead of that he had offered the rebels most favourable terms. What guarantee was there that Shivaji would observe even those terms, or that he might not win over Jai Sing to his side? All the clique of Shayista Khan's friends and supporters, urged on by his wife, fanned the embers of Aurangzeb's suspicions.

Soon after the cold letter of pardon, Shivaji received a second letter, phrased in very different language. "You are at present serving in Our Imperial camp. . . . In recognition of your services a handsome dress and a pretty little jewelled sword are sent to you herewith." The Emperor was little accustomed to the language of flattery, and from that sharp-tongued autocrat, references to "a pretty little jewelled sword" suggest something of a tigerish caress. A second letter was even more friendly: "We have a high opinion of you," it began, and then Aurangzeb's purpose was revealed. "Therefore we desire you to come here quickly and without loss of time. When we grant you audience we shall receive you with great hospitality and soon grant you leave to return."

On the face of it there was nothing unreasonable in Aurangzeb's desire. Like Louis XIV., the Moguls had always preferred to have the more powerful of their feudal nobles and tributary princes at court, rather than on their estates, where they would be exposed to temptation, with too much leisure in which to brood over fancied wrongs or trifle with ambitious projects. Even the superb Maharajas of Rajputana were required to wait upon the Emperor; only the ruler of Udaipur, the semi-divine descendant of the Sun-God, then, as to-day, the chief of Hindu princes, was excused attendance at court. Shivaji, so lately in arms against the Emperor, could hardly expect the same consideration as Udaipur. Nevertheless there was something odd about this sudden, almost fawning offer of hospitality.

Shivaji was in a dilemma. If he refused the Emperor's invitation he would provide an excuse for his arrest, and perhaps for his execution on some charge of renewed hostility, but if he accepted and went to Court he would be, in effect, a prisoner, hundreds of miles from his own land and people. No one who knew anything of Aurangzeb believed in the sincerity of his sudden change of opinion, nor could be satisfied by vague promises of a safe return.

As always when perplexity, Shivaji turned to his mother for advice. Jijabai reflected deeply, and at last reluctantly counselled acceptance of the Emperor's invitation. Next Shivaji consulted Jai Sing. He naturally advised Shivaji to go to court. He himself had been so fascinated by Shivaji that he believed a great future awaited him in the capital. The Emperor's suspicions would be lulled by that frank smile that lit a real beauty in the Maratha's lean face. And Shivaji, pleased by Aurangzeb's attentions and by the flattering interest of the courtiers, would forget his local ambitions and settle down to a life of service in the Imperial cause. Shivaji diffidently suggested that perhaps the invitation was a trap. Jai Sing at once offered his own son, Ram Sing, as a pledge for the good faith of the Emperor. "He shall accompany you to court and remain at your side." Ram Sing, who had shyly admired the Maratha ever since his arrival in the Imperial camp, supported his father's offer, delighted at the prospect of close companionship with Shivaji.

At last Shivaji consented. But he was filled with suspicion and foreboding. He made over his principality to his mother as Regent to rule in his place should he never return; and Jijabai, leaving her prayers and housewifery, took her place at the head of Shivaji's council table with the calm authority of a Macedonian princess. Then Shivaji took leave of his ministers, who wept bitterly as they embraced him. He cast what might well be his last glance at the yellow fields and violet hills of his native land, and mounting his horse, he set out on his long ride north, on one side of him his young son, Sambhaji, on the other Jai Sing's son, Ram Sing, and behind him an escort of Maratha cavalry.

CHAPTER FIFTEEN

THE Imperial Court was at this time at Agra. The country round this city was "exceeding well tilled and manured, being the best of India and plentiful of all things. It yields great store of poudered Sugar. Here all the way is set on both sides with trees, the most of them being Mulberry. Every ten or twelve miles, there are Serais built by the King, very faire for the beautifying of the way, for the memory of the King's name, and entertainment of travellers. There you shall have a Chamber and place to tye your Horses, also store of Horse-meat."[1] By such wide shaded roads, spending each night in the government-run guest houses, where, even in the hot weather, one had to sleep indoors, the doors being locked from sunset to sunrise, "for feare of Theeves", did Shivaji and his party come to Agra. This was a more magnificent town than Delhi, the traditional seat of Mussulman government, covering a far larger area and noted for the greater splendour of its private mansions. It had not been built to any plan like the last city of Delhi, nor was it fortified with regular walls, so that, in spite of its great size, it resembled a

[1] Richard Steele's *Relation.*

country town rather than a metropolis. Narrow streets wound their way between the tall stone houses of bankers and the palaces of nobles with arcades enclosing mango-shaded patios. There were gardens everywhere with "little groves of trees as Apple trees (though scarse),[1] Orange Trees, Mulberrie Trees, Mango Trees, Coco Trees, Figg Trees, Plantan Trees, theis latter in rancks, as are the Cipresse trees. In other squares are your flowers, herbes, etc. whereof Roses, Mariegolds to bee seene; French Mariegolds aboundance; Poppeas redd, carnation and white; and divers other sorts of faire flowers which wee knowe not in our parts, many groweinge on prettie trees,"[2] refreshment for the gardens being provided by "prettie conceited Artificiale Waterworkes." The English traveller, Finch, wrote of Agra: "It is so spacious, large, populous beyond measure that you can hardly passe in the streets. The Citie lyeth in the manner of a half-moone, bellying to the landward some 5 C. in length and as much by the Rivers side upon the bankes whereof are many goodly houses of the Nobility." Wandering at hazard down the narrow streets one came suddenly upon the Palace which rose "on the river side, built of square hewen redd stone. That part which sides towards the water lyes straight upon a ligne about a quarter of a mile,

[1] The apple-tree was first imported into India by Akbar from the orchards of Samarkand.

[2] Peter Mundy.

and comes rounding right into the Citie. Heere is its best prospecte, which is loftie and stately, garnished with handsome compleat battlements on the wall; above it appearinge divers of the Kings places of residence, some of whose upper coveringes are overlaide with Golde."[1] Mr. Finch considered that "the Castle is one of the fairest and admirablest in the East, some 3 or 4 miles in circumference, inclosed with a faire wall, about which is cast a great Ditch, over it Drawbridges."

Some of the courtiers had their own palaces at Agra, others quartered themselves on their friends or on rich merchants when the Court came there. There was no hereditary aristocracy in the Western sense, except the feudatory princes who paid homage for their dominions and held office under the Emperor. The other members of the Court circle were mostly officials whose eminence was due to the temporary favour of the Emperor, and such favour seldom outlasted one reign. There were, of course, a few families related by marriage to the royal family which exercised great influence, but there was some danger in too close a relationship of this kind. One was apt to be relegated to a distant province, or even to prison, as a precautionary measure. The atmosphere of the Court circle was fatalist and cynical. In former reigns when the Emperors were agnostic the court had been orthodox.

[1] Peter Mundy.

But in time a general scepticism had succeeded the earlier fanaticism; and whereas Akbar had been hated by the majority of his officials for his egocentric theosophy and Jehangir for his lazy toleration, Aurangzeb was now sneered at for his old-fashioned beliefs. But, as in all agnostic societies, superstition was rife. Astrology and sorcery were two of the most profitable professions. The most successful magician of the time was a Portuguese who, with a couple of old European books, some gabbled phrases, and immense self-assurance had convinced every one of his great powers as a Frankish wizard.[1]

The prosperity of the city had, during the reign of Shah Jehan, owed much to the large factories of Dutch and Armenian merchants trading in "broad-cloths, looking-glasses, gold and silver, laces and ironwares." The Dutch were particularly skilful in their relations with the authorities and "found it useful to have confidential persons near the court always ready to proffer a complaint against any governor or other officer who may have committed an act of injustice on any of the Dutch establishments."[2] Their former rivals, the English, had closed their factory during the reign of the late Emperor, probably because of the increasing lawlessness; even the main caravan route from Surat to

[1] Bernier. Even to-day Indian sorcerers often advertise themselves as "Europe trained."

[2] *Idem.*

Agra was constantly raided by bandits. In Agra was also a large Jesuit church, built in the time of Akbar. It had been notable for its campanile, whose bells were audible all over the city—unfortunately as it turned out, for the more fanatic Muhammadans became exasperated by this constant reminder of a foreign place of worship and successfully petitioned Shah Jehan for the demolition of the campanile. Now the public celebration of Christian festivals, which in Jehangir's time had included processions through the principal streets, was proscribed. Frowned on by the authorities, Christianity, which had been a court fad in the time of Jehangir, rapidly lost favour with the rich and the church was visited by few.

Outside the city was the tomb of Akbar, reminiscent in its details of Buddhist art. This was "placed in the midst of a faire and large Garden, inclosed with bricke walls neere 2 miles in circuit." Nearby was a palace where the women of Akbar's harem, each endowed in his will with vast possessions had had to end their days, "deploring their deceased Lord, so that this should be to them a perpetuall Nunnery." To the east, overlooking the river, was the Taj Mahal, the tomb built by Shah Jehan for his queen, then as now the resort of every visitor to Agra. But while to-day the Taj Mahal is a national monument, it was then a shrine. The inner chamber was only opened once a year and no heretic or atheist might enter. In the galleries and arcades that stretched round the gardens, alms were distributed to the poor three times a week, in accordance with Shah Jehan's instructions. For Aurangzeb was meticulous in the performance of such pious desires of his father. It was only in the matter of his father's continued imprisonment that his professions of filial devotion appeared insincere. But the world had already forgotten the deposed Emperor, who, in confinement in the Jasmine Tower, for seven years dragged out a miserable existence, sustained in his sorrows by Princess Jahanara. Indian sentiment has always been moved by the picture of the old Emperor and his devoted daughter who had once been the chief lady of the court, had worked against Aurangzeb and was now a humble suppliant for favours from her sister, the triumphant Roshanara. Popular artists have painted them sitting together in affectionate intimacy, on the balcony of the Jasmine Tower, gazing across the brown, slow-eddying river at the white loveliness of the Taj, the mausoleum that it had taken twenty-thousand labourers twenty-two years to build.

But some of the incidents of the ex-Emperor's captivity are more amusing than affecting. Aurangzeb, while greatly desiring his father's death, could not bring himself to order an act of direct violence. Instead he tried to frighten the old man to death by ordering his guards to beat kettledrums and gongs continually under his window, to exchange shots, shout war cries and break earthenware jars by throwing them against the wall. Shah Jehan was, according to court rumour[1] quite unmoved by this uproar and disappointed the hard-working performers outside his window by getting noisily drunk, dancing, singing obscene songs and shouting for the prettiest of his slave girls. Various attempts to poison him failed. Finally, if we are to believe contemporary gossip, his death came about through his own vanity and not through his son's patient malevolence. One morning when he was waxing his moustache in front of a mirror he saw in the glass two slave girls who were standing behind him making derisive gestures to each other in mockery of their master's feeble virility. This was a subject on which the old man was deeply sensitive. He at once ordered a large supply of aphrodisiacs. After taking an overdose of these he fell into so deep a stupor that, in Manucci's phrase, he could not even smell the smell of an apple. He never recovered consciousness.

Along the river bank facing the Taj were the mansions of the great nobles. One of these was Jaipur House, the palace of Jai Sing, to which his son Ram Sing came on a May evening in 1666 with Shivaji as his guest. A handsome building; the

[1] Manucci.

walls and ceilings were covered with gold leaf or painted with designs of flowers and fruit; in carved niches stood porcelain vases and flower bowls; the floors were spread with silk carpets under which were several thick mattresses to afford comfort to the feet—for then, as to-day, one shuffled off one's shoes at the door; the only furniture in the front rooms was a quilted bolster, covered with cloth of gold, velvet or flowered satin, running the whole length of one wall for men to recline against.

Three days after Shivaji's arrival the Emperor was to hold a Durbar and Shivaji was summoned for his first interview with Aurangzeb.

Ram Sing and Shivaji, attended by their retainers, rode to the main gateway of the Palace—and there dismounted—for only Princes of the Blood might continue on horseback into the Palace enclosure. Their arrival, as of every courtier of rank, was signalled by a flourish of trumpets from the band room over the gate, and a military march played by twelve hautboys, twelve cymbals and twenty pairs of kettledrums.[1] Proceeding slowly through the cavernous red archway they came out into the colonnade which led to the outer Hall of Audience. On either side were the almost legendary gardens of the Moguls, and the courtiers in their robes of flowered satin, clustering about the pillars covered with gold leaf, were not more magnificently

[1] The details of the Durbar are taken from Bernier and Thevenot.

adorned than the little tame deer that ran about the lawns with jewelled saddles hung with silken tassels and silver bells, and the Usbek hounds in coats of scarlet and gold.

Shivaji and Ram Sing were ushered by chamberlains into the Hall of Audience. This was a vast ante-chamber to the main palace, open on three sides to the royal gardens and hung with tapestries and carpets. Walls, ceiling and pillars were overlaid with gold leaf and powdered lapis lazuli. As Shivaji entered, he faced the great red wall dividing the Hall from the Imperial apartments. Half-way up this wall was the Balcony of the Throne, known as the Seat of the Shadow of God, on to which the Emperor issued from his private quarters. All eyes were turned to this balcony, and at noon, to the sound of trumpets and drums, the flowered curtain at the back of the balcony was drawn apart and the Emperor entered and took his seat on his throne, behind him the great peacock constructed of blue sapphires and pearls and over his head two umbrellas of red velvet sewn with rubies. The Emperor's robes were of white silk, his turban of cloth of gold, having an aigrette of diamonds and over his forehead an enormous topaz "of very high colour, cut in eight panels." Ranged round the Emperor, a troupe of eunuchs stirred the air with fans of yaks' tails and of peacock's feathers. Below the Balcony of the Throne was an enclosure surrounded by rails, reserved for the Gentlemen of the Household, feudatory princes and ambassadors of foreign powers. These were attended by servants carrying fans, fly-whisks and silver spittoons.

The question of admission to the railed-in enclosure was always a knotty problem of Court etiquette. "This red Rayle" wrote Hawkins, "is 3 steppes higher than the place where the rest stand. . . . At this Rayle, there are doores kept by many Porters, who have white Rods to keepe men in order. In the midst of the place, right before the King, standeth one of his Sherriffes, together with his Master Hangman, who is accompanied by forty other hangmen, wearing on their heads a certain quilted cap, different from all others with an Hatchet on their shoulders and others with all sorts of Whips." And to be expelled from the enclosure was the outward sign of loss of favour with the Emperor. So Hawkins, after a period of favour, fell into disgrace owing to the "bloudie Plots" of the Jesuits, and when he "made Arse or Petition unto the King . . . he not only denied me but also gave order that I be suffered no more to enter within the red Rayles which is a place of honour."

At the entrance of the Emperor all the courtiers, with the precision of a corps de ballet, bent their heads and crossed their hands upon their breasts, affecting to be overcome by awe, to be dazzled by the royal appearance.

Then began the slow ceremonial of the Durbar. First were led before the Balcony, to the sound of slow music, the elephants of state, painted jet black save for the heads, which were striped with scarlet. They were saddled with embroidered carpets hung with great silver bells and white yaks' tails. Beside each elephant of state walked two small elephants in far more sober attire, for they were supposed to be the retainers of the royal beasts. As each elephant approached the Balcony it bowed one leg, lifted its trunk and trumpeted in salute. There were three hundred of these elephants of state or, as Hawkins calls them, "Elephants Royall, which are Elephants whereon the King himself rideth; which when they are brought before him come with great jollitie, having some twentie or thirtie men before them with small Streamers. These Elephants Royall eat tenne Rupees every day in Sugar, Butter, Graine and Sugar Canes." The elephants were followed by antelopes and buffaloes, painted with alternate stripes of yellow and vermilion, their horns covered with gold leaf and gay with coloured streamers, and by panthers on gold chains. There were occasionally, if we may believe Mr. Thomas Coryat,[1] even unicorns in the procession of animals. Mr. Coryat assured his "most deare and beloved Friend, Master L. Whitaker," that he had actually seen two of these unicorns led before the Emperor. He

[1] Coryat's *Letters.*

had the grace to add that they were "the strangest Beasts of the World" and were only found in Bengal where all sorts of rarities abounded, it being "a place of most singular fertilitie." But Mr. Coryat was perhaps not the most conscientious of reporters. His main interests in Agra were two; his ambition "to have my Picture expressed sitting on an Elephant," and his lively appreciation of the low cost of living in the East ("I sometimes lived competently for a penny a day") so long as one avoided transaction with those "lewd Christians of the Armenian Nation."

Occasionally the Emperor permitted himself a remark. Instantly the eunuchs leaned forward to catch every syllable, and then bending over the Balcony railings they repeated the august comment to the Gentlemen of the Household, who were craning up on tiptoe in a flutter of excitement. As soon as they had mastered the Emperor's words, they extended their arms towards him, crying, "A miracle! A miracle!" (*Karamat*, *karamat.*)

After the animals had returned to their stables the Emperor reviewed his Guard. The cavalry rode past in fantastic uniforms, "the horses furnished with iron armour." Swordsmen engaged in mock duels and demonstrated their skill and the fine temper of their weapons by cleaving sheep clean through with a single blow.

At last the serious business of the Durbar began.

One by one the courtiers and officials, headed by the Prime Minister Umdat-ul-Mulk, were summoned before the Balcony by a herald. Advancing with slow steps, their eyes on the ground, they performed the *taslim*, the Salute to the Emperor. This consisted in placing the back of the right hand on the ground, and raising it slowly till one stood erect, and then placing the palm of the hand on the crown of one's head. The *taslim* had to be thrice repeated by each official who then made his offering to the Emperor, a gift of jewels, money or curious ornaments, arrayed on a gold tray. If the Emperor was satisfied with the quality and value of the gift he signified his pleasure by placing his open palm upon it. A eunuch then carried the tray through the doorway behind the throne.

On this 12th of May the machine-like regularity of court routine was disturbed by a disagreeable incident. After the Ministers had presented their gifts the herald cried, "Shivaji Raja!" Shivaji, with his son Sambhaji and ten Maratha officers, advanced to the silver railing of the enclosure below the Balcony, carrying a tray piled with two thousand gold mohurs. But instead of performing the elaborate Persian gestures of the *taslim* he salaamed thrice to the Emperor by bowing and touching his forehead with his open hand—which was the salutation he required of his own followers. There was a moment's silence in the Hall. The courtiers covertly watched their Emperor. Aurangzeb's face remained impassive. He accepted Shivaji's gift with an inclination of the head. Then he whispered to an official who descended from the Balcony and led Shivaji away from the centre of the Hall to the ranks of the lesser nobility. "This is your proper place in the court precedence," he said and left Shivaji there.

It seems certain that, even without Shivaji's omission of the *taslim*, the Emperor intended by deliberate insult to exasperate Shivaji into expressions of disloyalty which would furnish an excuse for revoking the safe-conduct. To place one whom the court herald had pointedly addressed as Raja among cavalry captains and petty barons was an obvious provocation. Shivaji's mortification was increased to find that he had to stand behind a Rathor officer who had once been signally unsuccessful in action against the Marathas. With a curious anticipation of Wellington's gibe at Marmont in the couloir of the Paris Opera-house, Shivaji turned and said to a neighbour, "It seems I must look at this Rathor's back. Of course, my men have often seen his back before."

Ram Sing, alarmed at the stir caused by Shivaji's remark, hurried to his side and tried to calm him, promising to intercede with the Emperor for the proper honours that were Shivaji's due. But

Shivaji refused to be pacified and continued to talk loudly and rudely, to the increasing consternation of the officials. Aurangzeb, however, ignored the interruption. Ram Sing, who knew well the Emperor's temperament and was far from mistaking his present silence for acquiescence, tried to excuse Shivaji's outburst. "He is a hill chieftain," he urged, "and knows nothing of court etiquette." The Emperor made no reply, but directed the ceremony of weighing against gold to commence. Of this ceremony the French traveller, Thevenot wrote[1] "The Balance wherein this is performed seems to be very Rich. They say that the Chains are of Gold and the two Scales, which are set with Stones, appear likewise to be of Gold, as the Beam of the Balance does also, though some affirm that all is but Guilt. The King, Richly attired and shining with Jewels, goes into one Scale of the Balance and sits on his Heels and into the other are put little Bales, closely packt . . . full of Gold, Silver and Jewels or of Rich stuffs . . . when it appears in the Register that the King weighs more than he did the year before, all testifie their Joy by Acclamation, but much more by rich Presents which the Grandies and the Ladies of the Haram make to him when he is returned to his Throne; and these Presents amount commonly to several Millions. The King distributes a great quantity of Artificial Fruit and

[1] Lovell's translation, 1686.

other knacks of gold and silver, which are brought to him in Golden Basons."

After this ceremony the Durbar came to an end and the courtiers, after a final obeisance, dispersed. Shivaji and Ram Sing returned together to Jaipur House, the Maratha still complaining of the insult offered him in open Durbar. Soon, however, he had further cause for complaint. Shortly after he had entered Jaipur House a detachment of cavalry rode up and surrounded the building. They were followed by foot-soldiers of the Guard and by gunners who trained cannons on every door of the house.

Now for the first time Shivaji lost all hope. He sank down upon a divan and burst into tears. His son Sambhaji came in to comfort him and Shivaji clasped him to his heart as though in a last farewell. But as time passed and the soldiers remained quietly on guard, it became clear that the Emperor had not planned Shivaji's immediate execution. He preferred to play with his victim, torturing him with suspense.

Though Shivaji was forbidden to leave the house and the investing troops were under the command of Polad Khan, the Chief of Police, yet Aurangzeb kept sending Shivaji polite little messages and even presents of fruit. Shivaji sent a message to the Prime Minister Umdat-ul-Mulk, reminding him of the safe-conduct granted him. Unfortunately that official was the brother-in-law of Shayista Khan, who from his exile in Bengal was intriguing for Shivaji's murder. So Shivaji received no reply.

His only ally in the Imperial household,[1] unknown to him, was one of Aurangzeb's daughters named Zinat-un-Nisa. She had been watching the Durbar through a lattice and she had fallen in love with Shivaji. "She was struck with the handsomeness of his person, admired his pride and haughty deportment," and indeed his independence and courage may have seemed remarkable in contrast to the machine-like routine of that Court. She interceded for him at the feet of her father; but we do not know her father's reply. Zinat-un-Nisa never married, but as the Begum Sahib or Princess Royal her influence in the Palace became very great. Many years later, when Shivaji's son had been trapped by the Moguls and tortured to death, Shivaji's grandson, also called Shivaji, was handed over to Zinat-un-Nisa to bring up as a Mogul courtier. The Emperor had intended the child to be made a Muhammadan; but Zinat-un-Nisa threw herself at Aurangzeb's feet and begged him not to disturb the child's religious beliefs and Aurangzeb unwillingly consented. In her devotion to young Shivaji Zinat-un-Nisa showed how the extraordinary impression made on her by the child's grandfather had been little affected by the passage of time.

[1] Orme, quoting from Dow, tells this story.

Ram Sing, too, was pleading continually for Shivaji's life and safety. At first Aurangzeb said nothing, and later asked coldly, "Why are you so interested in this affair?" Then, remembering Ram Sing's defence of Shivaji at the Durbar he announced, with grim playfulness, that he would appoint Ram Sing as Shivaji's jailer, responsible for his safe custody. When Ram Sing protested, Aurangzeb tried to alarm him by talking vaguely about his suspicions of all Hindus and threatened that if he had any more complaints from Ram Sing he would send both him and Shivaji to some fortress in Afghanistan.

Shivaji realised that the Emperor wanted to provoke him to some desperate action which would be the excuse of his murder. An official bulletin would record that he had been "shot while escaping." But instead of losing his head he began to oppose cunning to cunning.

The guards round the house were presently surprised to notice how cheerful and happy Shivaji had become. He joked with the soldiers on duty, sent presents to the officers and constantly remarked how healthy he found the climate of Agra—pleasantly dry after the depressing dampness of his native hills—how grateful he was for the Emperor's gifts of fruit and sweetmeats, and what a real relief it was to be rid of the endless round of statecraft and diplomacy, to be at ease as a gentleman of leisure in this delightful city of the civilised north.

It is not to be supposed that Aurangzeb was at once deceived by this sudden change from despair to carefree optimism. Through three long months they watched each other, the Imperial expert in dissimulation studying Shivaji's essays in acting. The summer wore on. The dust storms of June were succeeded by the thunder storms of July, with their accompanying discomforts of mosquitoes and malaria. But Shivaji showed no sign of impatience or distress. Spies watched him night and day, and reported to the Palace that he seemed to be as contented as ever. Even Aurangzeb's suspicions were at last allayed.

Shivaji now asked the Emperor if his wife and mother might come and live with him in Agra. Naturally the Emperor consented. A man would not offer his women-folk as hostages if he meant to escape. And Shivaji had left his mother as Regent of his possessions. To call for her without even troubling to nominate a Regent in succession to her showed that he had lost all interest in his little state. It was true that, in spite of Imperial permission, the women never seemed to arrive, but the delay might be attributed to the heavy rains in the Maratha country which made travelling difficult all through July and August. So Aurangzeb, perhaps wondering if all the tales he had heard of Shivaji's valour and cunning were only fables told by his officers to excuse their own failures, began to despise the prisoner he had at first thought so dangerous. Shivaji's next request confirmed his low opinion of Maratha spirit. The man suggested that all his escort of Maratha horsemen should be sent back to their homes. "I have no need for soldiers here," Shivaji explained. The Emperor shrugged his shoulders. He had been wanting to get rid of Shivaji's retainers and was glad that the suggestion came from Shivaji himself.

Now Shivaji was quite alone except for one or two servants. Alone in the Mogul capital, guarded night and day by picked men . . . there was nothing more to be feared from him. And he seemed to be settling down with genuine contentment into northern ways of life. He was learning Persian etiquette. He exchanged presents of sweetmeats and fruit with nobles of the Court, accompanying them with elaborate, if clumsy, compliments. He sent dishes prepared by his cook in the Maratha manner to the houses of the Mogul officials, and if they found the simple food of a southerner somewhat tasteless after their enormous pilaus, they recognised the courtesy that prompted the offer and in return sent him plates of savoury rice from their own tables.

At first all these baskets and plates and cauldrons and jars passing in and out of Jaipur House were carefully examined by the sentries, the Chief of Police himself superintending the search. But he and his men presently grew tired of turning over mounds of rice, probing about among piles of mangoes and jars of steaming soup; and they began to let the baskets and cauldrons (slung on bamboo poles and carried by porters) pass in and out of the house with only a perfunctory question to the servants or a peep under the lid of a basket.

Pilaws and birianis and kawftas—it was really very kind of the Mogul nobles to return Shivaji's gifts of humble Maratha dishes with examples of their own sumptuous fare. But Shivaji's stomach was unused to such a rich diet. In the middle of August he fell ill with some acute liver disorder attended by fever and cramp. The Mogul sentries could hear him groaning as he tossed in delirium. Physicians came to poultice him and shook their heads over his evident agony. They prescribed powders, rest and massage. He proved a good patient. He lay quietly in bed, took the various drugs without hesitation, allowed himself to be massaged. Once he roused himself to say that one should not put all one's trust in human aid and begged the sentries to let out two of his servants to buy some horses which he wanted to send as a gift to the shirne of Krishna at Mathura, the great centre of Hindu pilgrimage between Agra and Delhi. Hindu superstition, thought Polad Khan, but he told his men to let the servants pass. If any one had noticed how slowly these servants dawdled along the road to Mathura with their horses, he would probably have remarked that that was only to be expected of servants whose sickly master could not punish them for their slackness.

On August 19th, Shivaji felt much better. He had still to keep to his bed, but the cramp had almost gone. He remembered that according to Mogul etiquette one should send presents to one's friends on recovering from illness. So he announced he was offering two baskets of fruit to one of the Court officials. The Chief of Police raised no objection and when the baskets came swinging out of the house on their bamboo poles, the sentries at the gate neither examined the baskets nor searched the porters.

As soon as the porters were out of sight they set down their baskets. Out of one stepped Shivaji and out of the other his son, Sambhaji. The porters threw off their cloaks of coarse cloth. They were two Maratha officers who had stayed with Shivaji in the guise of servants, after he had sent home his other retainers. One other officer had done the same. He was called Hira. When Shivaji left Jaipur House in the basket, Hira lay down on Shivaji's bed, wearing Shivaji's clothes and his chaplet of pearls. He pulled the blanket up to his neck and turned his face to the wall as though the fever had returned; but one arm lay outside the blanket and on it was clearly visible Shivaji's bracelet and on one finger Shivaji's signet ring. The physician's assistant, a young boy who came daily to massage Shivaji for his cramp (Shivaji must have won him over either by a bribe or by the exercise of his charm) squatted down beside the bed and began to massage Hira.

Towards noon the guards noticed that the house was very quiet and they entered, only to find, as they naturally supposed, Shivaji lying once more helpless with fever. With muttered apologies they withdrew. In the afternoon Hira left Shivaji's bed, resumed his own clothes and walked out of the front door, accompanied by the young masseur. He told the sentries that Shivaji had sent him to buy something from the bazar, drugs and soothing ointments. Seeing the physician's assistant with him the sentries imagined he was going to get the materials to make up some prescription. They asked after Shivaji's health. Hira shook his head. "He has had a bad relapse. Do not disturb him. Please make as little noise as possible."

He then sauntered off towards the bazar and the silence of the long Indian afternoon settled over Jaipur House, over the empty rooms where remained no trace of the Maratha captives, and over the sentries drowsing at the gates.

Polad Khan, the Police Chief, who no longer thought it necessary to be present in person all day to supervise the guarding of Shivaji (he must always have considered such extraordinary precautions unnecessary) had gone home to enjoy his siesta. Without the spur of his presence the discipline of the sentries at Jaipur House had relaxed. It was not till evening, the grey, breathless, dust-laden evening of Indian August, that they began to stir.

After a time they became conscious of a strange quiet in the house they were supposed to be guarding. There were no footfalls, no sound of voices. As evening faded into twilight no lamps were lit. A dreadful suspicion deepened into more dreadful certainty when a feverish search of the house revealed that the helpless invalid had been spirited away. The soldiers ran with their tale to Polad Khan. He hurried to the Palace and flung himself before the Emperor. "Witchcraft," he stammered, "Witchcraft! . . . He has vanished, whether he has flown through the air or disappeared down into the earth we know not."

According to another account[1] it was Ram Sing (whom Aurangzeb, as will be remembered, had made responsible for Shivaji's safe custody) who had to break the news to the Emperor. He begged for a private audience. Appearing before the Emperor he made a profound obeisance. Then folding his arms he remained silent, his eyes on the ground. Aurangzeb was puzzled by his attitude, for Ram Sing was a favourite at Court on account of his good

[1] Manucci

humour and high spirits. He questioned him. At last in a low voice Ram Sing acknowledged Shivaji's escape. There was an awful silence. Aurangzeb raised his hand to his head, laid his palm on his forehead, and remained for a long time motionless, the expression of his face inscrutable. When he emerged from his reverie he deprived Ram Sing of his rank and property and banished him. No one but himself and his executioner could appreciate fully his exasperation. It was not only irritating to lose an important political prisoner. But he had just an hour before decided that, illness or no illness, Shivaji would be better out of the way and had secretly ordered his murder that night. . . .

Meanwhile Shivaji, with his son and companions, had passed through the Western gate of the City[1] and crossed the river in the ferry-boat without being questioned by any one. When they reached the far bank Shivaji took out a handful of money and giving it to the boatman told him to go and inform the Emperor that he had carried Shivaji and his son across the Jumna.[2] This was not an act of wild bravado. Shivaji was anxious to advertise the fact that he was travelling Westwards. The point of this will be seen presently.

Hurrying along the road to Mathura, Shivaji overtook the servants whom he had sent with horses

[1] See note at the end of the chapter. [2] Orme.

as an offering to the Krishna Temple. The whole party now mounted on horseback and galloped all night till they reached Mathura the following morning. Mathura is famous for its temples dedicated to the cult of Krishna. In one of them is a palm tree made of solid gold. Round most of the temples are monasteries, seminaries and lodging houses for pilgrims. Wide, cobbled courtyards surrounded by the cells of monks; pools of still, dark water coated with rose petals; heavy pylons carved with figures of gods and men and animals; and under the archways and through the narrow doorways an endless crowd of worshippers, Brahmans with shaven heads and robes of yellow or scarlet silk, students or novices in simple white, widows shrouded like ghosts, princesses in curtained palanquins and beggars in clamant hordes. At dawn all the multitudes of the faithful move towards the river whose waters lap the steps of the Krishna temple, and there, as the first light gleams, they perform the ritual of sun-worship, lifting handfuls of water, and scattering the sun-reflecting drops before them with the prayer, "Glory of the Sun, enlighten my understanding." Mingling unobtrusively with these crowds of preoccupied worshippers, the fugitives from Agra attracted no attention. In the cell of a friendly Brahman named Kashi, Shivaji and his companions changed their clothes. Shivaji shaved his head, cut off his moustache and beard, smeared his face with ashes and put on the yellow robe of a religious mendicant. At his waist was a begging bowl and in his hand a pilgrim's bamboo staff. The bamboo, however, had been hollowed out and, like Justinian's ambassadors in China, Shivaji carried treasures in his stick. His companions, too, dressed themselves as priests and wandering friars. In India this has always been a favourite disguise.

Shivaji had to leave his son behind. He was worn out by the long ride through the night. The Brahman, Kashi, offered to hide the lad in his own cell. He dressed him in Brahman clothes and gave out that he was his own son come to visit him.

So Shivaji and his companions set out once more on their travels.

They were hundreds of miles from the Maratha country. As soon as the alarm was given the Imperial couriers would be galloping down the great roads, warning all local authorities to be on the look-out for the fugitives. Now since Shivaji had sent some horses westwards and had apparently followed them himself, to judge from the boatman's report, the government naturally assumed that he was making a dash for the Maratha country by the direct route south-west through Khandesh and Gujarat. So Shivaji doubled back on his tracks and raced eastwards, risking the immediate danger of running into the arms of his pursuers.

In every town and village the alarm had been sounded; rewards were offered for Shivaji's capture and threats uttered against any who helped him. In one village he was actually arrested on suspicion and brought before the police inspector of the village, who put him through a gruelling cross-examination lasting far into the night. Towards midnight Shivaji broke down and confessed his identity, but judging the inspector's character with his usual acumen he offered him some jewels as the price of his freedom. The inspector accepted the bribe and let Shivaji go. It was a lesson that he must move with even greater care than before and now he travelled only at night and alone, his companions travelling by different routes.

At that time a Brahman named Nabha happened to be studying at Benares under one of the Chief Priests. He had of late become dissatisfied. He complained that his preceptors worked him too long and kept him short of food. He would have welcomed any opportunity of following some other occupation. One morning, before the sun had risen, he went down to the river bank and sat there alone, probably brooding over his grievances. The spires of innumerable temples were black against the greying sky; a few lights shone waveringly in an occasional shrine or under some tree where a panther-skin-clad ascetic repeated his prayers; the dim mist of dawn hung low over the swift-running river. As he sat there musing, a muffled figure came out of the shadows and, approaching him, said, "Will you perform the ceremonial ablutions for me and recite the dawn prayers?"

Nabha agreed and, in the chill and gloom, went through his Brahman's ritual for the stranger.

Suddenly the city was awakened by a number of trumpets and drums. The police watch rode down the streets, rousing the householders and proclaiming that Shivaji had been traced to Benares. The stranger and the Brahman looked at one another. The stranger said, "Open your hand," and placed in it nine large jewels. Nabha nodded. He turned away and began to pray as though nothing had happened while the stranger slipped away into the darkness. But that day the Chief Priests awaited their novice in vain. He left Benares and travelled to Surat where he bought a large house and set up practice as a physician. Many years later he confided in the historian Khafi Khan and told him the origin of his worldly prosperity.

Tramping and riding, Shivaji reached the shores of the Bay of Bengal.

Even in a small fishing village the noise of his flight had preceded him. When he tried to buy a horse, the horse-dealer became suspicious.

"What do you want it for?"

Shivaji offered him some gold coins. The man's suspicions were confirmed. "You must be that escaped Maratha to be so free with your money."

In despair Shivaji offered him the remainder of his money. Once again the avarice of another saved him. But now he was glad to escape alive, with no money left, without even the horse he had hoped to buy.

Wearily he turned back towards Central India. As he neared Indore he sought refuge in a peasant's hut, trusting to traditional Indian hospitality to avoid too many questions. He was welcomed as a poor wayfarer. His host's old mother hurried off to the kitchen to prepare supper. It happened that a body of Maratha irregulars had recently burst into Imperial territory. The village where Shivaji now rested was one of those that had suffered from their incursion. When the old woman came back from the kitchen she began to curse the Marathas for their depredations.

"As for that brigand Shivaji," she added, "I wish to God he had died in prison."

Shivaji asked her how much loss she and her family had suffered in the raid. A few months later, when he had reached his kingdom, he sent her a purse containing twice the sum of money at which she had computed her loss.

Shivaji's mother was still acting as Regent. She

have heard of Shivaji's escape in August but thereafter nothing was known of him except that the whole Mogul Empire was in a turmoil and that the authorities were searching for him everywhere. Four months passed and still no news came.

On a December morning she was sitting alone in her private apartments when a servant brought a message from a friar who wanted to see her. She nodded. A tattered and travel-stained mendicant was shown in.

Without looking up she said, "Yes, what is it?"

The mendicant said, "I have come on an errand to you," and fell at her feet.

Touched by the gesture she raised him up and for the first time saw his face.

It was Shivaji.

The news of Shivaji's return spread like lightning over the Maratha country. Night and day guns boomed, from every hilltop bonfires flamed and rockets shot up into the winter sky; the villagers abandoned themselves up to festivities; Shivaji's magic name was in every one's mouth, and every man who could voyaged to the capital and hung about the gates craving for a sight of the king returned from his captivity, to hear new gossip and detail of his extraordinary escape and perilous wanderings, to laugh at the thought of the stupefaction of the Moguls.

The Viceroy of the South, Maharaja Jai Sing, was in despair at Shivaji's return. As soon as he had heard of Shivaji's escape he wrote distractedly, "My anxieties are ceaseless. I have sent trusty spies in various disguises to get news of Shivaji." Now all his fears were confirmed. "That infernal Shivaji," he lamented, had returned, and "who knows what is in his heart?" He had been distressed by Shivaji's imprisonment, a breach of the Imperial safe conduct, and exasperated by the Emperor's action in holding Ram Sing responsible for Shivaji's custody. With the news of Shivaji's escape came also that of Ram Sing's disgrace and dismissal from Court. If the son had so signally incurred the royal displeasure, might not Aurangzeb vent his anger also on the father? Rumours came to him that Mussulman courtiers, jealous of the high office and enormous fame of the old Rajput, were accusing him of complicity in Shivaji's escape. This accusation was terrible to one of Jai Sing's loyalty. "May God give death," he cried, "to the man who cherishes the very thought of such an act of ill faith!" It is tragic that at the end of so long and distinguished a career in the service of the Empire Jai Sing's last months were clouded by fear and grief. "There is no medicine against Fate," the old man said and waited for a word from the Emperor. It came. Jai Sing was dismissed from his post and recalled to court. Broken with shame, unnerved by apprehension, Jai

Sing travelled slowly northward. But he never lived to face the Emperor. He died on the way. His son Ram Sing did not long survive him. He died of plague in Assam.

Though Shivaji and most of his companions (the latter travelling separately or in small groups) had returned safely, there still remained Shivaji's son Sambhaji who, it will be remembered, had been left behind at Mathura with a friendly Brahman. If the Imperial authorities found him, they would take revenge on him for his father's escape. So Shivaji resorted once more to his "stratagems." He began publicly to refer to his fear for Sambhaji's life, pretending to be ignorant of his whereabouts. Mogul agents reported that he seemed "very anxious about his son." Then he announced that he had received intelligence of Sambhaji's death. He wept bitterly and ordered all his followers to go into mourning. The Mogul's agents were completely deceived by this show of sorrow and assumed that the news must be correct.

A few days later Shivaji sent by a trusted servant a letter to the Brahman Kashiat Mathura, begging him to bring Sambhaji to Raigad. Still disguised as a Brahman lad Sambhaji set out with Kashi on his return to the Maratha country.

They had a narrow escape at Ujjain where a Mogul police officer, watching Sambhaji closely, came to the conclusion that his demeanour was hardly that of a priest's son.

"Is this really your son?" he asked Kashi. Kashi said yes, and began talking glibly about a pilgrimage to Allahabad where they had bathed in the sacred river and visited the temples, but how unhealthy they had found the climate there, unhealthy, that is, for Southerners, for instance Kashi's own wife who had fallen ill there and died, and so now father and son were returning mourning to their village.

The Mogul cut short his chatter with, "If he is really your son, let me see you both eating out of the same plate."

Now for a Brahman to eat with a non-Brahman is a gross infringement of the caste rules, only to be atoned for by expensive and wearisome penances. But Kashi, realising how carefully the police were watching his every expression, never showed for a moment his reluctance; and he and Sambhaji sat down to dine together from the same dish.

Convinced by this proof of kinship, the Mogul police released them and they reached Raigad without further adventures.

NOTE ON SHIVAJI'S CAPTIVITY AND ESCAPE

THERE is some disagreement among historians concerning the place of Shivaji's captivity. Earlier writers preferred Delhi, relying on Maratha sources. On the other hand Khafi Khan says Agra. It can hardly be doubted that the Muhammadan northerner would be better informed about local affairs than the Hindu southerners. Moreover, to most southerners even to-day, Delhi has a certain mythic quality as Rome to Europeans of the dark ages, so that it is often used as an expression for the Court of Government. Bernier (p.190) says that Shivaji went "to meet the *Mogul* at *Delhi*" but does not say that in fact the captivity took place there; anyhow, the whole story is dealt with in two or three lines, and Bernier shows himself (particularly in the fatuous suggestion that Aurangzeb himself engineered Shivaji's escape) ill-informed about the incident. Orme says Agra, but he is often inaccurate. Thus he relates that Sambhaji died during the flight. Apart from the historians, the person who should have known where the incident occurred one would suppose to be Shivaji himself. In his letter ordering a reward of twenty-five thousand rupees to be paid to Kashi for bringing Sambhaji he begins, "On leaving Agra . . ." Dr. Fryer, who is always careful and accurate, concludes his account with "'tis believed he (Shivaji) will hardly venture to Agra again."

With regard to Shivaji's route of escape Sir Jadunath Sarkar who gives the fullest account has fallen into a curious error. He writes, "Instead of moving due south-west from Agra, he travelled *eastwards* to Mathura. . . ." Now in spite of Sir Jadunath Sarkar's italics Mathura is and always has been west of Agra. Presumably this is the explanation of Sir Jadunath's slip: Most earlier writers had chosen Delhi as the scene of the incident and Sir Jadunath at first followed them. Later, however, he changed his view and substituted Agra for Delhi (from which Mathura is, in fact, east) without, however, troubling to correct the geographical details of Shivaji's flight. This, however, makes Shivaji's movements unnecessarily obscure. Obviously the point of a preliminary movement *west* to Mathura (a movement which he had well advertised) was to convince the authorities of his intention to follow the direct route to his own country, whereas in fact he turned back and raced eastwards.

CHAPTER SIXTEEN

SHIVAJI on his return from the north had taken over the reins of government from his mother and the Council of Regency. His position with regard to the Moguls was curious. Officially he and his state were at peace with the Empire; but that peace might be regarded by Shivaji as having been broken by his imprisonment and attempted murder, and by the Moguls by Shivaji's triumphant return to his Capital. Actually neither side desired war, at any rate yet. Jai Sing had been succeeded by another of the great Rajput feudatories Jaswant Sing, Maharaja of Jodhpur.

It is curious that Aurangzeb, after his dismissal of the far abler Jai Sing on the grounds of his son's sympathy with a fellow Hindu, should have sent another Hindu to command the Army of the South. But his suspicions of all his Muhammadan generals and their possible ambitions made him rely, in spite of his bigotry, on Hindu generals, in the same way that the Caliphs at Constantinople relied on Phanariot officers. But now he made the fatal mistake of a divided command that Jai Sing had taken preliminary measures to avoid. He made his son, Prince Muazzam, Viceroy of the South, in charge of the civil administration, while Jaswant

Sing commanded the armed forces. The Emperor hoped that each would spy on the other and thus he would be kept fully informed about the doings of both. As he noted, "The greatest pillar of Government is the immediate knowledge of everything that happens in the kingdom." However, Jaswant Sing was a smooth-tongued courtier. He flattered the Prince and kept him supplied with polo ponies and wrestling boys to solace his ennui in exile from the capital. In return the Prince allowed Jaswan Sing effectual control over both army and administration.

Jai Sing, as soon as he heard of Shivaji's return, had written in agitation to the Emperor that Shivaji must be caught again at all costs. If the old Rajput had been shocked by the breach of faith involved in Shivaji's imprisonment he realised that now questions of honour must be waived. Embittered and desperate, Shivaji would be now twice as dangerous an enemy as before. He urged an immediate resumption of the war and the recapture of Shivaji by force or guile. Before his recall his troops were in action against the Marathas.

Jaswant Sing was a man of different calibre. He was selfish and pleasure-loving and his experience had been that of a courtier rather than a field officer. Moreover he had met Shivaji at Agra and like all "who passed under the wand of that magician," had become his warm admirer.

The war, resumed by Jai Sing, now remained in a state of suspended animation for a year. Finally, in February, 1668, a new treaty was drawn up with terms very different from those accepted by Shivaji from Jai Sing. Most of the twenty-seven forts, garrisoned by Mogul troops in accordance with that earlier treaty, were returned to Shivaji, of the forts round Poona only Purandar and Sinhgad, the Lion Fort, being retained by the Imperialists.

Shivaji addressed a letter to the Emperor to which Aurangzeb replied patronisingly: "Compliments. We hold you in high esteem. After reading your letter we have dignified you with the title of Raja. You will receive this distinction and show greater capacity for work." Considering the events of the last few years this note seems a pleasant exercise in the art of face-saving.

It was not only the Moguls to whom Shivaji's reappearance in the Maratha country was an unexpected blow. The Bijapur authorities, especially when they heard what favourable terms Shivaji had received from the Moguls, became alarmed. They were afraid that, without any distraction on his northern front, the baleful glance of "that Inhuman Butcherly Fellow" might turn south. They hastened to treat with him and as the price of Maratha non-aggression Shivaji received as tribute from Bijapur three hundred and fifty thousand rupees.

For two years Shivaji remained at peace with both his Mussulman neighbours. After the alarms and excursions of his earlier career this sudden passivity surprised every one. Almost incredulously, and with an undertone of suspicion, the English factors wrote to one another. "Sevagy is very quiet." Again and again this refrain is repeated in their letters. "The country all about at present is in great tranquillity. Shivaji keeps quite still," and "Shivaji is quiet, not offering to molest the King's country."

He employed these years in the reorganisation of his kingdom. Taxes were reduced and the land rate on all estates devastated by the Mogul invaders was suspended. So firmly had he laid the foundations of his authority on a just and equal land tenure and on the centralisation of both justice and administration (as opposed to the erratic feudal systems at work in neighbouring territories) that his country recovered from the losses of the last war with surprising ease.

The secret of the prosperity of his State as well as of the devotion of his subjects was that, following the example of his old tutor Dadaji in his administration of the family estate round Poona, Shivaji introduced a sensible and just system of taxation. The land tax was levied, not on any hypothetical considerations of a man's probable wealth or the fertility extent of his land, but on the actual state of his crops each year. The land was divided into three classes:

rice; hill tract; and garden land. On rice land the tax assessed was thirty-three per cent. of the yield, payable either in kind or in cash. In garden land (that is, orchards, palm-groves, etc.) an amount equal to half the produce of each tree was levied. Hill country was very lightly taxed. If these assessments seem high it should be remarked that they were far lower than those prevailing then in any other state in India. Above all the taxes were regularly collected and remitted direct to the State; there was no intermediary class of tax-farmers nor any feudal landowners who could rack-rent their tenants. All land belonged to the Prince and, unlike other Indian States, no territories were made away to great nobles as a reward for services whether in battle or at court. The revenue system of Shivaji is the basis of the present agricultural administration in British India.

Under Shivaji the State was administered by a Council of Eight. These were appointed by Shivaji himself. They had in effect only the position of secretaries to the Prince. This Council had grown out of the body of clerks who worked in Dadaji's office administering Shivaji's lands round Poona. As Shivaji rose from being a petty landowner to the position of an independent ruler so the functions and position of these clerks and their successors were enlarged. After his return from Agra he added a Chief Justice to his Council. All his councillors were Brahmans, with the exception of the War Minister, who was a Maratha.

When Shivaji was present in person in his capital these councillors had little authority, though it appears that treaties with foreign powers had to be signed not only by Shivaji himself but by every member of his Council. Nevertheless when he left his kingdom, as on his visit to Agra or on a long military expedition, he would select the Council of Regency from among the members of his standing Council. It is safe, however, to assume that the ministers of justice and of ecclesiastical affairs suffered very little interference from Shivaji in their administration. Questions of Hindu law and religious tradition are so involved in their details and distinctions that only a Brahman expert could unravel their complexities; and Shivaji was not a scholar in an age and country where the atmosphere of the educated classes resembled that of the Schoolmen in fifteenth century Europe. It was inevitable that for lack of other intellectuals Brahmans should predominate among Shivaji's ministers; but it was unfortunate. One day the power of the Brahman officials would grow so great that a Brahman Mayor of the Palace would eclipse Shivaji's descendants.

A problem that faced him from the beginning was the employment and provisioning of his army. In time of peace the upkeep of a standing army would be a heavy burden on a poor State; at the same time the army's discipline and organisation had been the work of years. All that labour would be lost once the army was dispersed, and no one imagined that the present peace would last long. Shivaji's partial solution of this problem was typical. Playing on Jaswant Sing's admiration for him he proposed that, as a symbol of the new friendliness between the Marathas and the Empire, a body of Maratha horse should enter Imperial service. The proposal was eagerly accepted. Shivaji chose out a thousand picked troopers, the nucleus of his cavalry, and despatched them to the Viceroy's Court. There they remained for two years "feeding at Mogul expense" as the Marathas gleefully commented, while the Imperialists congratulated themselves on their diplomatic tact.

Unfortunately this pleasant little arrangement annoyed the Emperor. As soon as he heard of it he began to suspect that there must be some secret triple alliance between Prince Muazzam, Jaswant Sing and Shivaji. The ever-recurring memory of his own method of ascending the throne made him scrutinise anxiously the behaviour of each of his sons. In order to test his son's loyalty he sent Muazzam a letter directing him to entice Shivaji to his palace, seize him and send him to Delhi, where the Court was now in residence. There would be no escape this time.

Muazzam, who trusted his father as little as his

father trusted him, had spies among the Emperor's servants and one of these reported to him that this order was on the way. The Prince, though lazy and incompetent, had some sense of honour and refused to be a party to deliberate treachery. Moreover, he had met Shivaji with Jaswant Sing and had been charmed. He sent a secret runner to warn Shivaji not to accept any Mogul invitations. At the same time he advised the commander of the Maratha cavalry at his court to leave quietly, at night. When the messenger from the Emperor arrived, Muazzam was able to make a show of obeying his father's instructions, knowing that Shivaji was aware of the plot for his capture.

It was clear, however, that war would soon break out again. The Emperor ordered new regiments south under the capable but erratic Afghan, Dilir Khan, whom he associated in the command with Muazzam and Jaswant Sing. At once dissensions broke out in the Imperial Camp, both Muazzam and Jaswant resenting deeply Dilir Khan's appointment and the airs of superior dignity that he affected. The three Mogul generals quarrelled in a confused and desultory manner. Prince Muazzam, it is difficult to understand why, save for the general atmosphere of suspicion and distrust which had invaded Aurangzeb's Court, believed Dilir Khan to be a spy appointed by the Emperor to watch Muazzam.

Dilir Khan, a rough and brutal warrior, insulted the careful courtier Jaswant Sing. All three wrote busily complaining of each other to the Emperor, who, for his part, had to deal with a sudden Persian invasion and a Pathan rising at Peshawar. The position was very different from that at the time of Jai Sing's campaign. With a divided command and no common plan of action the Moguls drifted into war with the Marathas, who at once took and maintained the initiative.

The first Maratha objective was the recapture of the few forts in the Maratha country still garrisoned by Mogul troops. The first attack was launched on Sinhgad, the Lion Fort, which lies towards the south of Poona. On clear days its vast cliffs of basalt are reflected in the still cold water of Khadakwasla Lake; on grey days of cloud its summit is lost in the clouds, its dark shoulders seeming to sustain the sky. A natural fortress, and if properly defended almost impregnable. The walls were built above natural cliffs with fifty feet of sheer face of rock. There is but a single gate which bristled with iron spikes and was flanked by great towers.

At the renewal of the Mogul war it was held by a thousand picked troops, Afghans, Arabs and Rajputs, under a captain named Udai Baun of whose bodily strength and feats of arms the minstrels sing ballads in western India to-day. It is said that even Shivaji was at first nervous of attacking the Lion Fort and had to be urged on by his mother. A Maratha ballad[1] relates that she was sitting one morning at the window of her palace in Pratapgad combing her hair with an ivory comb. The sun rising over the hills to the east shone on the ramparts and precipices of the Lion Fort. For a moment she rejoiced in the spectacle. Then, as she remembered that it was still in Mogul hands, her face darkened with anger. She called a servant and ordered him to ride to Raigad and call her son. Shivaji obeyed her summons and came to his mother's palace, riding his black mare. He asked her why she had called him so urgently but she made evasive replies and then suddenly challenged him to a game of dice. He was at first surprised but, to humour her, he agreed. He lost the game and then smiling, said:

"What will you have as forfeit from me?"

Pointing towards the window she said, "Give me the Lion Fort."

"But it is still in Mogul hands."

She shrugged her shoulders and repeated, "I want the Lion Fort."

He offered her any of his fortresses that she should choose.

"But I don't want them, I want the Lion Fort."

At last Shivaji agreed. Then he sat silent for a long time. To take the Lion Fort by storm was a

[1] Translated in Kincaid's *Ishtur Phakde*. See also Acworth's *Ballads of the Marathas*.

formidable task. Only one of his captains, he thought, was capable of such a feat. This was the gay and gallant Tanaji who had accompanied him in all his campaigns, had been with him in Agra and followed him in his escape. Shivaji sent to call Tanaji. When the messenger arrived Tanaji was at his young son's marriage but he abandoned the ceremonies and at once set out. On the way a coppersmith bird flew out of a tree and pursued him with its dull cry. This is an omen of death, but Tanaji laughed and pressed forward. He arrived at the palace at nightfall and asked what orders Shivaji had for him.

"It is not I but my mother who needs you," Shivaji said, turning to Jijabai. She rose and lifting a five-wicked lamp she moved it slowly over Tanaji's head in sign of blessing. Then she said, "Will you take the Lion Fort for me?" Tanaji took off his turban and laid it at her feet with, "Lady, you shall have the Fort."

In the morning he left the palace and collecting a band of hillmen rode towards Sinhgad. Stationing his men in hiding in the woods he went forward alone in disguise as a peasant and questioned some villagers at the foot of the hill who told him all they knew about the approaches to the Fort. That night, a cold clear February night, Tanaji and his men stole up to the foot of the walls, which, naked and smooth, without crevice or foothold, rose heavenwards like a flight of spears. Aloft, remote and high as birds of prey, the sentinels paced slowly from bastion to bastion and turret to tower.

Tanaji ordered a servant to bring forward a box which he carried on his shoulder. He laid it on the ground and out came a ghorpad, the hill-iguana of western India. These iguanas are so surefooted that they can ascend a smooth and vertical surface, and so strong that they can, as the Marathas proved, bear the weight of a man.[1] This was a ghorpad of especial size and strength. It was called Yeshwant.

Tanaji began to praise and flatter Yeshwant. He painted Yeshwant's head with red lead as if it were the head of an image in a temple: he hung his own pearl necklace round Yeshwant's neck and bowed to Yeshwant as if to a prince. Then he tied a rope ladder round Yeshwant and told him to run up the wall. The ghorpad obeyed and darted up the sheer face of stone. But half-way up Yeshwant stopped and began to shudder. It was a hideous omen. Tanaji's men clustered round him and begged him to abandon the enterprise. "The ghorpad's fear is a sign of your own death," they urged. But Tanaji laughed and said, "I have given my promise, I cannot turn back." Then he turned and shouted up at Yeshwant, "Get on up, you wretched lizard, or I'll cut you up and serve you in a stew."

[1] This fantastic method of siege-operation became a favourite one with the Marathas, and to-day several noble families bear the name of Ghorpade, bestowed on their ancestors for their skill in the training and use of ghorpads.

Yeshwant, in natural alarm, ran up the rest of the wall and disappeared over the stone crenellation. The rope-ladder dangled down the fifty feet of wall. A young hillman climbed quietly up and made the rope fast. An Arab sentry emerged from a tower and stood listening. Seeing the hillman bending over the rope he advanced. But Tanaji, from below the wall, bent his bow and shot the sentry dead. Then with three picked men following him he swarmed up the rope ladder, his face hidden in a fold of his turban and a *tulwar*, or curved sword, between his teeth.

But the sentry's fall had not passed unnoticed. Voices rose in the guardhouse, torches were lit and soldiers stumbled drowsily out into the chill February night. But Tanaji was already over the edge of the wall. Some Afghan guardsmen saw him. They rushed at him and cut him down. As he fell he still shouted encouragement to his men and then, rolling over, died.

The Marathas poured over the wall yelling their battle cry, "Hurr! Hurr! Mahadev!" Though there were but three hundred of them and the garrison one thousand, the surprise was complete. The Arabs and Afghans fought with desperate courage and when the struggle turned against them the remnant flung themselves from the walls. Of the Rajputs, a few, fearfully wounded, surrendered. In the battle the thatched roofs of the garrison's barracks caught alight from a flung torch and a great tongue of flame sprang up into the sky. Shivaji, gazing anxiously with his mother from her palace window, saw that sudden flare across the wilderness of hills and turning to Jijabai said, "You have your fortress now."

But Tanaji's men took little joy in their victory. They stood round their fallen captain, weeping. Gently they laid him on a rich bed and bore him down the hillside while the guns of the fort above, now worked by Maratha gunners, roared homage to the hero, kettledrums rattled and the great gourd-drums boomed mournfully. Shivaji met the cavalcade and, at once realising what had happened, burst into tears.

"I have won the Lion Fort," he said, "and lost my Lion."[1] He ordered masons to erect a monument to Tanaji on the highest point of the Lion Fort and sent heralds with drums and ochre banners through all his villages to acclaim the desperate bravery and noble death of Tanaji. To each member of the storming party who followed Tanaji he gave a silver bracelet and a gift of money.

Immediately behind Sinhgad and on the other side of the pass to the south is the fortress of Purandar, that fortress whose heroic defence against Jai Sing

[1] The original Marathi is "Gadh ala, Sinh gela." Shivaji is admired by Marathas for his "bitter laconisms."

had been the last incident before Shivaji's submission to the Moguls. This was attacked after the Lion Fort, the storming party being led by Suryaji, Tanaji's brother, and brilliantly captured. In a very short time Shivaji had expelled the Moguls from all their forts in the Deccan. The Mogul Army of the South was almost immobilised by the increasing quarrels between the three commanders, Prince Muazzam, Jaswant Sing and Dilir Khan. Dilir Khan became convinced that the Prince intended to poison him and departed from his camp "on the plea of illness," and wrote to the Emperor accusing Muazzam of designs against the Emperor's life. Aurangzeb sent his Grand Chamberlain south to investigate the various charges and counter-charges, but these were by now so involved that the puzzled Chamberlain was unable to make up his mind who was in the right and in his report he (as an English gunner serving under Prince Muazzam contemptuously reported to the President of Surat) "played the Jack on both Sides." Affairs in the Imperial camp were, in the words of the Bombay factors, "so confused that we cannot write them."

The Marathas were not slow to take advantage of these circumstances, and in March the English factors were writing, "Shivaji now marches not as before, as a thief, but in gross with an Army of 30,000 men, conquering as he goes, and is not disturbed though the Prince Muazzam lies near him."

It was in vain that the Emperor charged his generals, bitterly rebuked Muazzam, ordered the Viceroy of Gujarat south with fresh troops. Shivaji's troops poured in a flood over Imperial territory and many towns and villages, while nominally professing subservience to the Emperor, entered into negotiations with Shivaji, buying exemption from Maratha raids by payment of what became known as *chauth*, that is, an annual sum of money amounting to one-fourth the value of the harvest. Similarly, in the decline of the Byzantine Empire, whole districts east of Brusa and Nicea bought exemption from Ottoman raids by tribute and presently became, without overt conquest or formal rectification of frontiers, incorporated in the Ottoman Empire.

CHAPTER SEVENTEEN

IN September Shivaji prepared a second attack on Surat. This time he advanced, not as before in secret and relying solely on the speed of his horses, but deliberately and openly with an army of fifteen thousand. On the news of the Maratha approach the Indian merchants fled panic-stricken from the city. The English cleared their warehouses and sent most of their property to Swally on the coast. The city had recently been newly fortified at the Emperor's express order. But when, on October 3rd, Shivaji opened the assault, the Mogul garrison put up a poor resistance. The new walls were easily cleared of defenders and the Maratha horse poured into the city. Once more a Mogul Governor proved his unfitness for his position by retiring into the citadel and remaining quietly behind its ramparts while the Marathas looted the city.

The first object of the Marathas' attention was the Tartar Serai. Most of the great trading nations of the East had their own Serai in Surat; the Turks, Persians and Tartars. One may gain some impression of the interesting activity in these great buildings, half store and half hotel, from the Tartar Serai still existing in Srinagar to-day. There the merchants from Turkestan, little wizened men with round fur caps and heavy ear-flaps, arrive with their blue carpets and great uncut sapphires. They huddle together on the rickety stairways, blinking like sleepy parrots; they peer over the carved balustrades and chatter at the windows overlooking the swift-running waters of the Jhelum; and the grave Kashmiri traders, hook-nosed and bearded, with white turbans and long-sleeved white coats, come down the river in their canopied boats to chaffer with the Tartars. The Tartar Serai at Surat in that October of 1670 housed an unusually distinguished guest, the King of Kashgar, a connection by marriage of the Emperor Aurangzeb. He had been dethroned by his own son but was able to leave Turkestan with most of his treasures. He occupied his exile by a visit to Mecca whence he was now returning, travelling in great state with "a vast Treasure in gould, silver, rich plate, a Gould Bedd and other rich furniture."[1]

In order to attack the Tartar Serai it was necessary to cross the French concession. The French merchants took fright and offered to let the Marathas pass through their quarters if they were assured of immunity. The offer was, of course, eagerly accepted. The English Council reporting disgustedly on this transaction wrote of the French, "They never shott off a Gunn, though at first being strong in Menn, they Vapoured as if they would have

[1] Hedges' Diary.

fought the whole Army themselves." The Marathas then attacked the Tartar Serai. The Tartars resisted successfully till evening; then under cover of darkness the King of Kashgar escaped with his staff and family to the shelter of the citadel leaving his treasures and "Gould Bedd" behind.

Meanwhile the English Council, which had moved to Swally, although their goods were safely out of Surat, decided to defend their buildings in the city. As they wrote, they felt they ought to preserve the English factory from mauraulders in order "to maintaine our honour and that of the Nation (which wee had hitherto reputably preserved) from any Scandal that might be cast upon us of deserting the Towne in Time of Danger." So they sent thirty English seamen under the command of Mr. Streynsham Master who "cheerfully undertooke the charge" and marched into Surat to meet, as he said, whatever "Divertisement" he might.

This admirable Englishman appears to have been as admired by his countrymen as by Indians. Mrs. Oxendeane of Deane, when sending to her brother-in-law in the Company's service in India "a crevat and cufs and riben of the newest mode with a border of lace for your night-cap" added in her covering letter, "I believe 'tis a great satisfaction to you sometimes to see and be with Streynsham Master. . . . He is so wise and experienced a Person." He evidently had a deep sympathy for

Indians, particularly for the country folk whom he described as "so meeke, gentiele and charitable." His sense of humour is attested by his letters; whether he is describing the converts of the Jesuits as "Rice Christians, that is those that profess and owne the Name of Christianity for Sustenance only" or commenting on the disturbance caused by an English soldier who (still further confusing the impressions of Christianity prevalent among the Indians of Bombay where a Protestant administration had so recently succeeded a Catholic one) set up as a religious teacher on his own and "Pretended the light of the Spirite which moved him to Preach. But the Deputy Governour did not thinke it convenient to have the like liberty and therefore took hold of him and clapt him in Prison where after a short time he came to a soberer understanding."

The day after Streynsham Master had reoccupied the English factory with his sailors a band of Marathas attacked the building but "found such hott service from our house, having lost many menn, that they left us." The following day they reappeared, their "Captain of Brigade calling to speake with Mr. Master from the Wall. . . . This Captain tould Mr. Master the Raja, or Sevagy, was much enraged that we had killed so many of his menn and was resolved on revenge." This message was delivered on his own responsibility for Shivaji, as he showed subsequently, had no desire to become seriously embroiled with the English, whom he always admired and liked. But whether authorised or not the ultimatum had no effect on Streynsham Master who replied, "If they offered violence the English were resolved to defend their house to the last Mann and would sell their Lives deare."

For two days they had a respite. They stood waiting at the walls, the fair-haired, ruddy-faced young English sailors, in the hideous heat of a Surat October. On the fifth a third party of Maratha arrived at the gates of the English factory, "casting out threatening Speeches, but Mr. Master stood in soe resolute a Posture," that the Marathas retreated.

Shivaji, who now for the first time seems to have interested himself in the English factory, had his troops recalled from that quarter and sent to the English a message of "soe reasonable a rate" that Mr. Master replied with a present of "Scarlett, Sword-blades, knives, etc." Shivaji then invited two Englishmen to visit him in his tent. When they arrived he went out of his way to be pleasant to them. "He received them with the Piscash, in a very kind manner telling them that the English and he were very good friends and putting his hand into theirs[1] he told them that he would doe the English noe wrong."

The English factory was not molested thereafter.

[1] A gesture of great affection and esteem from a Hindu, who never shakes hands at greeting.

Only one English sailor had been shot in the exchanges between English and Maratha over the factory walls. He was not one of the Company's servants but "belonged to the King of Bantam's ship called the *Blessing*." This sailor must have left the ship on which he was employed to help his comrades in the factory. Ships from Bantam (in Java) arrived in considerable numbers at Surat and they were often manned by English sailors, who had won a great reputation in Java, not only for their qualities of seamanship, but because they "never offered any wrong to the meanest in the Towne and were generally beloved of all the better sort; they would say it was not so with the Flemings, nor with no other Nation."[1] The factory at Surat depended largely on Bantam for its spices, in particular for *Lignum Aloes*, a wood casting forth a most delectable Odour; Civet of a deep yellow colour, somewhat inclining to the colour of Gold; and Muske, which ought to be of colour like the best Spicknard, that is of a deep Amber colour, and of so strong and fragrant a Smell that to many it is offensive, and being tasted in the mouth pierceth the very brain with the scent."[2]

On the evening of the fifth the Marathas withdrew from the town and marched leisurely southward. The Mogul commander, Daud Khan, who had been hurriedly despatched by the Viceroy to intercept

[1] Scot's *Discourse of Java*. [2] John Saris' *Relation*.

the Marathas, detached a body of cavalry to harass Shivaji's rearguard while with the main body of his infantry he blocked the Nasik pass to the south. Shivaji turned suddenly on the Mogul cavalry and cut it to pieces, and then crossing the Sahyadri mountains fell on the rear of Daud Khan's army in the pass and overwhelmed it.

Meanwhile at Surat the confusion was frightful. The Imperial authorities, venturing out of the fort after the Maratha departure, were unable to restore order; villagers came in from the country to pillage and Mr. Master found that the former attacks by marauding bands of Marathas were more easy to deal with than the flood of refugees who, astounded by the success of the English defence, poured into the factory grounds. "Most of the eminent Merchants, Moores, Armenians, Cuttarees and Banians were ffled hither under our protection." Even the Muhammadan population expressed the utmost bitterness against the feebleness of the Mogul administration and joined in the general praise of the English who were the heroes of the day. The son of Haji Said Beg, Surat's richest merchant, whose house the English had defended during the former sack, "Declared his Resolution with an Oath that he would goe with his family to Bombay" so as to be under English administration. His example was followed by many other traders, and while Surat never recovered from this second sack, Bombay materially benefited.

It is perhaps worth adding that the Englishmen of that century were not only admired for their courage but also for their courtesy. The Council had caused a "Paper Publikely to be affixed in the House for the information of all Persons" that "if any of the Company's Englishmen abuse the Natives, they are to be sett at the gate in irons all the day time."

Although the English had been lavishly praised by the authorities in Delhi for their conduct during the first sack of Surat, they received no honour on this occasion, for the Court was seriously annoyed at the comparisons made openly between English discipline and Mogul ineptitude. So the Imperial authorities contented themselves by spreading rumours that the English must have been in league with Shivaji and must be Maratha agents and that the attack on the factory was a carefully-staged "blind." This idiotic suggestion deceived no one.

However, if Mr. Master received no marks of honour from the Emperor for the protection he had given to so many of the Emperor's subjects, he was gratified by a medal struck in his honour by the Council with the fine Latin inscription, "*Pro meritis contra Sevageum.*"

CHAPTER EIGHTEEN

SHIVAJI'S successes continued throughout the winter of that year and the spring of the next. The English were bewildered by the rapidity of his movements. The Bombay authorities wrote, "Where he aims we cannot tell or imagine. He is always bound upon some desperate design."

Even the Portuguese began to fear for their possessions. His southern frontiers marched with those of the Estado da India and every now and then he would visit his border forts "changing his men and putting in fresh provisions and ammunition." He swung round to the south of Goa and there, as the English reported, "built a Castle upon a very high hill from which he may very much annoy those parts."

Dr. Dellon, a French physician visiting Goa, wrote, "This Sevaji is a most Potent Prince. He has managed his affairs with much Prudence as to have Established himself, in spite of his Enemies, in all these Territories and has made himself so Dreadful to his Neighbours as to have made the city of *Goa* Tremble at his Approach. His Subjects are *Pagans* like himself. But he tolerates all Religions."[1]

[1] Dr. Dellon was, of course, interested in the question of toleration, for he came into conflict with the Inquisition in Goa.

By threatening a third attack on Surat Shivaji induced the Moguls to move most of their forces in Central India westwards to cover Surat. But the threat to Surat this time was only a feint designed to draw off troops from his North-eastern frontiers. As soon as the main Mogul armies were trailing westward he burst into Central India and overran Khandesh.

From Delhi the Emperor despatched a new generalissimo, Mahabat Khan, a veteran of the previous reign, with reinforcements of forty thousand. This army, advancing down Central India, at first pressed back the Marathas. The Mogul advance was, however, slow. The elderly generalissimo was attended not only by a number of clients and friends but by four hundred selected Afghan dancing girls. Further reinforcements reduced still further the pace of the advance and after several months all that the English factors could report of Mahabat Khan's operations was that "he hath taken four castles," while "Sevagy bears himself up manfully against his enemies . . . and his Flying Army will constantly keep men in alarm." Early in 1672, in a long, confused battle outside Salher town, the Moguls were first held and then broken by a brilliant cavalry charge. Only two thousand men from the Mogul army escaped. Twenty thousand fell in battle or surrendered. To the wounded prisoners Shivaji was as chivalrous as ever. He tended their wounds and when they recovered he sent them and the other prisoners to their homes with handsome presents. Besides great numbers of prisoners the Marathas captured six thousand horses, one hundred and twenty-five war elephants and all the treasure chests of the enemy. As the Surat factors wrote, "He (Shivaji) hath forced most Generals who with their armies had entered into his country, to retreat with Shame."

Aurangzeb, exclaiming bitterly against the continued success of the Mountain Rat as he still called Shivaji,[1] appointed yet another Viceroy, Bahadur Khan, to command against Shivaji, but the spirit of offensive had passed from the Moguls to the Marathas. Only a few years before, it had been the aim of the Imperialists to force the Marathas into a pitched battle in which they would be bound to be defeated. Now it was the Imperialists who shrank from battle.

The new Viceroy after a few manœuvres which were contemptuously described by Captain Gary[2] of Bombay as "attending Sevagees Motion but affecting little materiall against him," settled down to build a line of forts and blockhouses to defend Imperial territory against Maratha raids. Many of the Imperial officers began to treat with Shivaji,

[1] Orme.

[2] A naturalised Greek, who had once been in Portuguese employment. Mr. Orme called him "a busy man, of much vanity, intrigue and plausibility."

others deserted openly, others devoted themselves fatalistically to the pleasures of the table and the harem, expecting every day to be ejected by the Marathas from their positions.

A vivid picture of the demoralisation of the Mogul army in the Deccan is given by Dr. John Fryer, who visited some of their forts when Bahadur Khan was Viceroy. He found the soldiers indifferent and cowardly—"he that runs fastest is the best soldier; besides, their Arms are kept so bright, they are afraid to handle them for fear of soiling them. Their Leaders are good Carpet Knights, loving their Buchannos better than the Field." The soldiers' wages were fourteen months in arrears and they would crowd round the Commander's house, "by their salam to refresh his Memory of their Pay." It is hardly to be wondered at that they showed little interest in the interminable and unsuccessful war. "If Seva Gi brings any Power, they betake themselves to Flight."

The officers, resigned to a conviction of ultimate defeat, made themselves comfortable in their palaces and consoled themselves for their exile from Delhi by the luxury of their living. One such officer received Dr. Fryer in "a verdant Quadrangle of Trees and Plants, he, the Mogul officer, being enclosed in a Seat of State, boulstered up with Embroidered Cushions, smoaking out of a Hubble bubble; afore whom lay a rich Sword and Buckler with a Crescent Moon instead of Bosses, his Page bearing his Bow and Arrows, much after the Turkish manner. . . . All the Floor was spread with a soft Bed, over all a fine white Calicut; the Pedestals were Massy Silver."

In case such luxury had not sufficiently impressed the foreign visitor, two singing men then entered and commenced a song in praise of Dr. Fryer's host, to whom they attributed all the virtues and graces. Dr. Fryer was not impressed. He considered the singing-men to be "Fawning Knaves," and contented himself with quoting Seneca on flattery.

Presently Dr. Fryer was shown round the harem which contained four wives and three hundred concubines. The ladies pretended to be overcome by shyness at the entry of the foreigner and ran about fluttering like birds, covering their faces with their hands; but Dr. Fryer noticed that they continued to stare at him between their fingers. Hearing his guest was a physician, the Mogul officer insisted on having one of his wives, whom Dr. Fryer found to be "a Plump Russet Dame," bled. When not ministering to the officer's pleasure or being experimented on by foreign doctors, the ladies appeared to Fryer to spend their time in sewing and eating confectionery and pickles. When Dr. Fryer asked the officer why, since he was supposed to be at war with the Marathas, he was making no move against them, he replied that "'twas a work of more pains to reduce Seva Gi, than was represented, in respect of his Situation," and then wandered off into a long tirade against the Viceroy, Bahadur Khan, who, he said, did nothing at all except demand bribes. If this was typical of the *moral* of Mogul officers at this time Shivaji's successes are scarcely surprising.

As a pendant to Fryer's interview with a Mogul officer it is amusing to compare the visit of a contemporary Mogul gentleman to an Englishman in Bombay.

"Abd-ar-Razza had been friendly with an Englishman formerly at Hyderabad and this man kindly invited me to visit him in Bombay. I put my trust in God and went to the Englishman. When I entered that fortress I noticed on each side of the road . . . young men with sprouting beards, handsome and well cloaked, holding fine muskets. As I went on I passed Englishmen with long beards, of equal age and similar accourtements. Further on were Englishmen in brocade with white beards. I saw English children, pretty and decked with pearls on the rims of their hats." He reached his host's house and found him "seated on a chair. He wished me Good Day, their usual form of salutation. Then he rose from his chair, embraced me, and signed to me to sit down on a chair opposite him. After a few kind enquiries, our conversation turned upon different things. Everything he said was in a kind and friendly spirit. When the interview was over, he offered me entertainment after their fashion but I was glad to escape."

Having reduced the Mogul armies to a policy of inert defensive Shivaji suddenly turned east and advanced against the Kingdom of Golconda, which although a Mussulum state had prudently remained neutral throughout the long struggle of Bijapur and the Empire against Shivaji. Its neutrality did not save it from a demand for submission and tribute. Hastily the King of Golconda offered two million gold pagodas as tribute. The death of the King of Bijapur in the same year gave Shivaji an excuse for interfering in the affairs of that dilapidated kingdom and adding some of its territory to his own state.

He was now supreme in Southern India; to his co-religionists he seemed the Hindu rival to the Muhammadan Emperor in the North; and he decided to give a dramatic exhibition of his increasing power and authority. He announced that he would have himself crowned King of Hindu India, with the same rites that had attended the coronation of the old Emperors of India when all India was Hindu

PART FOUR

KING

CHAPTER NINETEEN

THE coronation was celebrated at Raigad in June, 1674. Every preparation was made to invest Shivaji's capital with new splendour befitting the occasion. New palaces and rooms of state were erected, were consecrated by the singing of traditional hymns, the burning of sacrificial fires and libations of holy water. In the audience hall a new throne was raised, surrounded by figures of tigers, lions and elephants and carved round its base with the thirty points of the compass in symbol of Shivaji's new imperial claims. In long trains from every part of India eleven thousand priests and one hundred thousand visitors journeyed towards Raigad, where they were entertained as Shivaji's guests for four months. From Benares the greatest of the Brahmans of that sacred town, Ganga Bhat, voyaged southwards in great state to perform the coronation ceremony. He was met by Shivaji and his ministers, who dismounted at his approach and conducted him by slow stages to Raigad.

The ceremonies lasted nearly a month. First Shivaji visited the temple of the Mother-Goddess at Pratapgad. He presented the shrine with an umbrella of pure gold, forty-two pounds in weight. Then, accompanied by a few followers, he entered the temple and passed many days in vigil and prayer. While prostrate in prayer before the altar he fell into a trance and from his mouth a faint thin voice, which those present declared must have been that of the Mother-Goddess herself, began to prophesy the future history of the Maratha state, the final collapse of the Mogul Empire, the entry of the Marathas into Delhi, the twenty-seven generations' rule of Shivaji's descendants and finally, the voice added, "The sceptre shall pass into the hands of a strange people with red faces."

By a curious chance an embassy from a people with red faces was even at that moment on its way to Shivaji's court, an English deputation from Bombay. They passed through the wooded country at the foot of the hill country; amused by "the busy Apes, the Forlorn hope of these declining Woods," which, "deeming no place safe where they beheld us, made strange Levaltoes with their hanging Brats from one Bough to another, chattering an Invasion"; and noticing in the Maratha troops they passed that the man's appearance was "distinguishable from the Moguls . . . peculiarly by their Hair appearing on both Ears under their Pucheries or turbans."

Shivaji being absent from Raigad, the English envoys were received by one of his ministers, Narainji Pandit, whom they found to be "a Man of Prudence and Esteem." They presented him with a diamond ring and his eldest son with two mantles. Shivaji had not known of the approach of this embassy when he left Raigad for Pratapgad and had made no arrangement for their reception; and, the town being crowded, they could not find accommodation, but had to live in a tent which they found uncommonly hot. As soon, however, as Shivaji returned he invited them into his "Castle" and gave them an interview, assuring them that they "might trade securely in all his Countries without the least apprehension of Ill from him." The details of the proposed commercial treaty had to be postponed till after the coronation, and the English envoys wandered about Raigad for a fortnight.

Surrounded by Hindu nobles in white muslin and shaven-headed Brahmans in togas of yellow or scarlet silk, those English merchants must have offered a strange contrast with their periwigs and feathered hats and laces and buckled shoes. We are so accustomed to think of all Oriental costume as gorgeous and exotic, that it is difficult to imagine the astonishment with which the comparatively soberly dressed Marathas must have regarded the peacock extravagances of Restoration costume. We know that even the luxurious Moguls, at their first meeting with Dr. Fryer, "admired the Splendour as well as the Novelty of our Europe Dress, asking my servant if I lay in them."

Another cause of surprise to the Marathas was the size of English appetites. We know that Shivaji himself only had one meal a day and that, as the English complained, was "only cutchery, a sort of Pulse and Rice mixed together, and boiled in Butter." Any one who has glanced over a menu of Stuart meals will appreciate the disgust of the English merchants at so meagre a diet. They complained finally to Shivaji, pointing out that they "had been used to feed on good flesh." Shivaji was anxious to oblige his guests but there was no meat available except goats' flesh and with this the English had to be content. They ate half a goat a day to the wonder of the Court. One is reminded of Mr. Gandhi's early conviction that the English must be inherently superior to the Hindus for no one but supermen could eat so much.

While the English were grappling with yet another difficulty about their food—for they insisted on having the goats' flesh roast and not "stew'd, bak'd or made into Pottage"—the ceremonies of Shivaji's coronation continued. His mother, Jijabai, now over eighty years of age, was brought before the palace in a litter. Shivaji publicly prostrated himself at her feet and she blessed him. Then began the long penances for all sins that Shivaji had, consciously or unconsciously, committed. For three days he continued in vigil and penance. At last adjudged free from sin by the priests, he was invested by the Arch-Pontiff, Ganga Bhat, with the Sacred Thread, the badge of the Twice-Born, and in his ear was whispered the Invocation to the Sun which only the Twice-Born may learn. Now in imitation of Mogul royalty he was weighed against precious metals and jewels, spices and wine and fruit and brocades, all of which were distributed to the Brahmans.

At the conclusion of this ceremony a little pantomime had been arranged to amuse the crowds. An artificial lake had been excavated but remained empty till a sluice-gate at one end should be opened. A man, supposed to be a magician, was to strike the ground, and, the sluice-gates then being opened, it would appear as though the magician's wand had called water from the rock. Unfortunately the magician's antics alarmed a rough Maratha infantryman, who, mistaking his gambollings and wavings of the wand for some attack on the King, drew his sword and cut the magician down. Shivaji was distressed at this sad end to the innocent pantomime and, calling his treasurer, ordered a piece of land and a generous pension to be given to the magician's family.

For seven days before the coronation the priests burnt sacrificial fires, fasted and prayed.

On June 6th the rites of the coronation proper began.

Clad in a white robe, crowned and garlanded with flowers, Shivaji entered the great hall of his palace, his queen-consort Soyra beside him, their robes being knotted together in token of their union. Behind Shivaji came his mother and his son Sambhaji. Then followed his eight ministers, each carrying a gold vessel filled with holy water. He approached his throne, which was covered with a canopy of cloth of gold from which pearls hung in festoons, lotus blossoms of gold and emerald being thrown among the crowds during his slow progress across the hall. He mounted the throne and every gun in the city boomed homage; from fort to fort along all the ghats Maratha guns answered the guns of the capital; from the plains guns in every Maratha outpost took up the loud salute, so that over every mile of country where Shivaji's writ ran people were aware of their ruler's coronation. Sixteen Brahman women advanced towards Shivaji on his throne and flashed lamps before his eyes and swayed them over his head to ensure good fortune. Then Shivaji rose and put over his simple white dress a heavy robe of purple embroidered with gold, and in place of the chaplet of flowers he put on a turban hung with tassels of jewels. The pontiff Ganga Bhat raised above his head the pearl-studded gold umbrella of imperial sovereignty, the soldiers clashed shield on spear and the crowds shouted and cheered.

Then descending from his throne Shivaji walked across the hall and mounted an elephant of state hung with gold-stitched carpets and went in procession through his capital. From every window women showered flowers and coloured rice on his head and waved lighted lamps. The banners of victorious regiments waved over the procession, waved in the sudden gusts of wind that blew over the town, waved again a mounting pall of thunder-cloud, the gold and silver tassels shining metallically in the last rays of the sun that was soon to be eclipsed by the first storm of the monsoon.

To-day, though the palace is in ruins, the traditional site of Shivaji's throne is marked by a mound and no one approaches it save barefoot, and men of low caste may not approach it at all.

After the coronation ceremonies the English envoys were formally received by Shivaji. After the usual pomp of presentation they exposed the purpose of their embassy. They complained of Maratha raids on English factories in Hubli and Rajapur; they asked permission to trade freely in Maratha territories with a maximum import duty of two and a half per cent. which was the amount now levied by the Imperial authorities in Surat; they requested the restoration of English ships cast away on Maratha shores and the free circulation of English coins in Shivaji's state.

Shivaji was conciliatory and reasonable. He gave the English ten thousand pagodas as compensation for damage suffered in a Maratha raid on Rajapur, but declined to accept their estimate of the damage at Hubli. With regard to wrecks he pointed out that these were traditionally the property of the coast fisher-folk but he promised to safeguard the persons of any English sailors on board such wrecks. As to English coinage he was glad to have it circulating in his state. His own mint could not turn out coins of the same purity and technical quality as Mogul coins. Indian Maratha coins of this period are of very poor execution. Shivaji's own name is spelt in no less than eight different ways on coins struck by his own mint. And the method of minting was primitive. In the mint "a certain quantity of silver of the required test was handed over to each man who divided it into small pieces, rounded and weighed them, greater care being taken that the weights should be accurate than that the size should be uniform. As the seal was larger than the piece of silver all the letters of the inscription were seldom inscribed."[1] So this request as well as that relating to import duties Shivaji "willingly conceded, embracing with much satisfaction our Friendship, promising to himself and Country much Happiness by our Settlement and Trade." The minister, Narainji Pandit, who had accompanied

[1] Bom. Gazetteer Vol. XVI., 429.

the English envoys proceeded further to utter "Expressions of great Kindness for our Nation." The English then presented Shivaji with a ring and he bestowed on Mr. Oxendon a robe of honour.

These pleasing exchanges were interrupted by a petition from a very old man who announced that all he wanted was to have a look at the Englishmen. He was, he explained, the butcher who had provided them with their goats' meat during their stay in Raigad. He lived at the foot of Raigad hill but hearing that the Englishmen were soon leaving he insisted on climbing the hill and seeing them in the flesh. Being brought before his English customers he stood staring at them for some time in silent awe. So these were the men, he said, who in such a short time had eaten more meat in a few days than all the rest of his customers put together during several years. . . .

A few days after Shivaji's coronation, while the winds howled down the streets of Raigad and monsoon rain beat upon the palace walls, Jijabai fell ill, lay peaceably reflective for a while and then prepared for her end. She had lived to see her son, whom she had brought forth in loneliness and poverty, crowned Hindu Imperator and it seemed as though she desired nothing further from life. She issued orders for all her goods to be distributed to the poor. On the fifth day of her illness she quietly died. Her body was burnt at Raigad and the ashes taken and cast into the Ganges.

A second English embassy visited Shivaji in the following year of which one of the members left the following account. "The Rajah came on the 22nd March about midday, accompanied with Abundance of Horse and Foot and about 150 palanquins. So soon as we heard of his near approach, we went out of our tent and very near met him. He ordered his palanquin to stand still, called us near him, seemed very glad to see us and much pleased that we came to meet him and said that, the sun being hot, he would not keep us now, but in the evening he would send for us. . . . The next day the Rajah came. He stopped his palanquin and called us to him. When we were pretty near we made a stop, but he beckoned with his hand till I was close up with him. He diverted himself a little by taking in his hand the locks of my periwig and asked us several questions. . . . With him we continued about two hours which was most part spent in answering many of his questions. At length we presented him our paper of desires, translated into the country language, after which had been read to him, with a little pause, seriously looking on us, he said that it was all granted us."

Nevertheless these cordial relations were disturbed by the Company's refusal (the factors presumably suffering at that moment from one of their periodic attacks of scruple) to supply Shivaji with "fifty Great Ordnance and two great brass guns," on the grounds that "so public an action as that must needs provoke this king" (Aurangzeb); and by a Maratha raid on Dharangaon where the Company had a factory which suffered some damage. Shivaji, however, refused to pay compensation as he claimed that the factory had been looted by "Vagabonds and Scouts without order or the knowledge of his General."

The Surat Council raged. "So long as that Pirate and Universal Robber lives, that hath no regard to friend nor foe, God nor man, there can be no security in any trade in his country."

However, after a "strict debate" relations improved and the Bombay council wrote complacently to Surat, "He hath confirmed all. A hundred *khandi*[1] of betel-nuts is sent us on account of our demand for satisfaction."

In spite of many disagreements the English seem always to have liked "our Neighbour Shivaji." As the Bombay Council wrote, "We dare say if he hath a kindness for any Nation it is for the English."

[1] Bags.

CHAPTER TWENTY

FOR two years after his coronation there was a lull in Shivaji's activities. He had loved his mother as he never loved any other woman, he relied constantly on her advice and experience and her death was a great blow to him. His health, impaired by his ceaseless energy, began to fail and in 1676 he fell seriously ill. He recovered but the naturally ascetic temper of his mind became more and more evident. He declared his intention of abdicating, and, as he had wished to do so many years before, living as a religious mendicant. Dissuaded from this, he would nevertheless disappear from his palace and wander alone in the woods or sit in peaceful meditation beside a forest pool or under a great tree. He abandoned the soft couch which he had adopted of recent years and slept always on a peasant's bed of string and wood.

With his mother's death his private life became clouded with anxiety and unhappiness. His first wife, Saibai, a gentle affectionate creature, was long dead, and her son the Heir-Apparent Sambhaji, who had accompanied Shivaji to Delhi, was growing up into a passionate, reckless man, impatient of his father's control. The present queen-consort was Soyra, a woman with the presence and character of an Agrippina. She wished to supplant Sambhaji with her own son, Rajaram, and gave Shivaji little rest by her ceaseless importunities and intrigues. She was right in her assumption that Rajaram was far better fitted to succeed Shivaji than the eldest son; and in fact, after Sambhaji's death (he was caught by Aurangzeb and, perhaps out of spite for his earlier escape with his father, put to death with awful cruelty) it was Rajaram who ascended the throne and reigned gloriously. But her obsession with this purpose disturbed the whole palace and embittered the relations between Shivaji and Sambhaji.

Recovering from his illness at the end of 1676 Shivaji seemed suddenly fired with new and youthful vigour. He set on foot preparations for the last and greatest of his campaigns. Whether in a start of inspiration or after long hours of meditation on his comfortless sick-bed, he conceived the idea of establishing a new stronghold of Maratha power in the south-west corner of India. Perhaps he remembered Jai Sing's campaign and realised that if the Moguls could produce another commander as able as Jai Sing in later years when the Marathas had no Shivaji to oppose them, the verdict of the recent years of war might be reversed. In spite of the Maratha successes and the apparently dispirited immobility of the Empire there was still no doubt as to which was the stronger power, could all the resources of the North be harnessed to the struggle. In manpower alone the superiority of the Empire was impressive. When Aurangzeb in person led his Grand Army south in his last campaign he commanded half a million men; and in artillery the Marathas remained always inferior till the collapse of the Empire and the diversion of the wealth of the North into Maratha coffers sent the foreign gunners and soldiers of fortune hurrying to seek service under Maratha chieftains. Geographically, the new Maratha state was peculiarly exposed. A solitary independent Hindu state, its frontiers were enclosed on all sides by Muhammadan territory; the Empire, Golconda, Bijapur. These two last might be militarily weak and, in present practice, little more than tributary states; but they had still great wealth, particularly Golconda, and if they came under the full control of the Empire (on whose action the rise of Maratha power made them peculiarly dependent) their territory would become the bases for flanking movements against the Maratha country. In fact, in Aurangzeb's last campaign the reduction of Golconda and Bijapur to complete submission was conceived as a necessary part of the general design to restore Imperial authority over the southern territories of India. It is a measure of Shivaji's military talent that at the moment of his apparent triumph he was particularly concerned to ensure his kingdom against future reverses.

Along the south-east coast of India lies the province of the Carnatic, noted to-day, as in the time of Shivaji, for its temples and its rich fields; an enclave of Hindu life almost untouched by Muhammadan influence; the enormous black shrines with their overdramatic, almost Pergamene sculpture, the courtyards and garland-scented colonnades thronged with Southern Brahmans with their square heads and heavy features and taste for brilliant colour, their slow, emphatic walk and the trident of Vishnu startlingly white against their high, dark foreheads; the endless fields of rice; the tapering palms moving in a moist wind. The Carnatic had been nominally under the control of Bijapur, the chief prince of the district, the Raja of Tanjore, professing fealty to the Sultan. But there had been little effective control, and at intervals, military expeditions were necessary to reclaim even the semblance of submission.

Shivaji's father, Shahaji, had, while in the service of Bijapur, commanded several such expeditions and as a reward had been nominated Governor of the Carnatic. After his services in securing a reasonable peace from his rebellious son Shivaji, his Governship was reaffirmed and on his death his son Vyankoji[1] was appointed to succeed him. Vyankoji was an undistinguished person and Shivaji had paid no attention to him till the plan of his last campaign

[1] Son, it will be remembered, by the second wife he married in Bijapur.

occurred to him. As a pretext for the grandiose expedition he intended, he suddenly claimed that Vyankoji ought all these years to have been sharing his Governorship with Shivaji for, by Hindu law, all property left by a man at his death devolves equally on his sons. Vyankoji, relying on the distance of his residence, Tanjore, from Shivaji's kingdom and on the many miles of Bijapur and Golconda territory lying between, proved unaccommodating. Shivaji, with a show of virtuous indignation, announced his intention of reclaiming his rights by force.

The moment of the expedition was well chosen. The northern armies of the Empire were involved in a wearisome struggle on the north-west frontier with rebellious tribes of Pathans.

Aurangzeb himself was engaged in quelling a rebellion in Rajputana. His increasing bigotry had alienated all his Rajput officers. Even the supple courtier Jaswant Sing, who died in 1678, dictated on his deathbed a letter to the Emperor in which he said, "God is the God of all mankind, not the God of Muhammadans alone. To vilify the religion or customs of other men is to set at naught the pleasure of the Almighty."[1] Now the Rana of Udaipur, the semi-divine prince, the chief of Hindu rulers, had drifted into rebellion. As with all Rajputs who struggled with the Moguls, the ancient traditions of Hindu chivalry were a grave disadvantage.

[1] Orme.

Aurangzeb's army was penned in a narrow defile where provisions ran short and the Rajputs only had to wait to receive the surrender of their terrible enemy. But with a courteous message the Rana withdrew his troops and let Aurangzeb return to his base. On another occasion Rajputs raided the Imperial camp and carried off Aurangzeb's favourite wife, the Georgian Udepuri (who, it will be remembered, caused him such distress by her addiction to drink). The Rana "received her with homage and every attention" and soon "sent her back to the Emperour accompanied by a chosen escort; but Aurangzeb, who believed in no virtue but self-interest, imputed the generosity and forbearance of the Rana to the fear of future vengeance and continued the war" and "destroyed all the objects of Hindu worship and every dwelling." The commanders of the southern Mogul armies had for some time only acted on the defensive against Maratha raids and their chief emotion on hearing of Shivaji's proposed campaign was relief that, two Maratha chiefs being embroiled in civil war, the pressure along the Southern frontier provinces would be relaxed. Shivaji turned this indifference into benevolent neutrality by secretly sending a huge bribe to the Mogul commander-in-chief. All through the autumn of 1676 Shivaji's preparations continued; a large expeditionary force was recruited, the fort garrisons were strengthened and a Council of Three was nominated to govern the kingdom in Shivaji's absence.

At the beginning of the new year he set out from Raigad with seventy thousand men, the largest Maratha force that had yet taken the field. He crossed Bijapur territory without resistance and arrived at the borders of Golconda. There he waited while his envoy at the Golconda court negotiated for a free passage for the Maratha force. It is not surprising that the king of Golconda was alarmed at the proposal. But he was helpless to resist. In spite of the splendour of its court and capital and the affection with which the amiable Persian dynasty was regarded by its subjects, Golconda was a very weak kingdom. The Mogul Emperor was fond of demonstrating the helplessness of Golconda by constantly demanding presents, especially of anything curious and unusual by which the king of Golconda set any store. On one occasion he demanded an elephant which had attained a certain celebrity by falling in love with a girl.[21] And Monsieur Bernier noted that "Aureng-Zebe's ordinary ambassador at the court of Golconda issues his commands, grants passports, menaces and frightens the people," while "the Dutch presumed to lay an embargo on all the Golconda merchant vessels in the port as a protest against the King because he prevented them from taking possession of an

[21] Manucci.

English ship, and even the Portuguese, wretched, poor and despised as they are become, scruple not to menace him, the King of Golconda, with war."

The wealth of Golconda, which gave it the exterior signs of power, was derived largely from the famous diamond mines of Colloor. Even these were worked in a haphazard and casual manner typical of all the administration of the state. William Methold, an Englishman who visited these mines at the beginning of the seventeenth century, found that thirty thousand labourers were employed in them. "Some of these were excavating the soil; others were carrying it away in baskets; others were drawing off the water by a tedious and laborious method (for these barbarians are not acquainted with any machinery), lifting it in vessels from hand to hand. . . . The soil is generally of a reddish colour, streaked with veins of yellow and white chalk and lime. When it is hardened and dried by the sun they break it with stones. They then sift the dust that remains; and in this operation they discover the gems, sometimes in greater, sometimes in less numbers. Not unfrequently they find none, and thus lose their labour and time."[1]

A second important source of revenue was the state monopoly of alcohol, especially the palm liquor, toddy. The brothels, more numerous than in any other Indian city, were the distributing

[1] De Laet.

centres of toddy, for the prostitutes could only retain their licences if they persuaded their clients to drink a certain amount of liquor and thus contribute to the State's revenue.[1] There were more than twenty thousand prostitutes in Golconda.

Each had to obtain a written licence to ply her trade and her name and address were entered in the book of an official called the Deroga. In street after street they stood at the doors of their houses, and when night fell their figures were outlined against bright candle-light. They were notably loyal to the dynasty and often showed their gratitude for state protection by giving free singing and dancing exhibitions outside the royal palace. Once when the king entered the city on a festive occasion he was welcomed not by the customary elephant of state, but by nine prostitutes inside a circus imitation elephant—a triumph of collaboration, one imagines, to judge by the difficulties of the two-man horse turn of the modern music-hall.

From its diamond mines and liquor monopoly the government drew a huge revenue and the aspect of the capital was very magnificent. The name, synonymous in the West with fabulous wealth, attracted many European adventurers. There was no army such as the Moguls for them to volunteer in, but they made a considerable business out of pretended conversions to Islam. One Robert Johnson

[1] These and following details from Tavernier.

"turned Moore, and lived there and was circumcised and received seven shillings and sixpence a day from the King and his diet at the King's table; but eight days after his Circumcision he died."[1] Another Englishman was, however, undeterred by this signal example of divine disapproval, Robert Trully, who had been first an employee in the English factory at Agra and had then set up on his own as a musician and composer (what kind of music can this contemporary of Purcell's have provided for Mogul concert-goers?). However, this new venture proved unsuccessful and he wandered south, "carrying with him a German for his Interpreter, offering both to turn Moores. Master Trulley had in his Circumcision a new name given, with great allowance from the King." The German, however, having arrived in the subordinate rôle of interpreter, was obviously rated by the king as one of inferior social status and thus of less value as a convert. He was treated with little consideration and in disgust "he returned to Agra and serveth a French man and goeth to Masse again."[2]

The population of the Golconda kingdom was entirely agricultural, peaceable south Indians, almost all Hindus of low caste, submissive and easy to govern. But there was no reservoir of military force to preserve the kingdom against foreign attack and the only foreign policy of the Golconda kings

[1] Withington's *Tractate*. [2] *Idem*.

was to satisfy their neighbours by regular money payments. For some years past Golconda had been paying tribute to the Moguls and to the Marathas. Fortunately the kingdom's wealth was such that both these disbursements were easily borne and the Golconda tradition of magnificent building continued without pause. A rich country with fine crops, abounding in orchards and in lakes full of fish, which, according to Tavernier, had "only one bone in the middle which is most delicious food." The men dressed, Tavernier remarked, in robes of "3 or 4 ells of Calicut. They wear their hair very long and tie it in a knot upon the top of the crown like the women, who have as headgear a piece of linen with three corners. The nobles do not wear scimiters like the Persians, but broadswords like the Switzers, as well for a thrust as a blow, which they hang by a girdle."

The reigning King, Abu Hussein, destined to be the last of his House, the last ruler of an independent Golconda, a cultured Persian gentleman of pleasant manners and artistic tastes, asked for nothing better than to continue in expensive peace with his neighbours and devote himself to his dilettante interests. Melancholy and lacking in vitality, his life had been saddened by a domestic tragedy. He had been out hunting one day when he saw a pretty shepherdess by a forest pool. He followed her home and bought her from her parents in exchange for several villages.

"Although of lowly birth," Manucci reported, "and of a somewhat black colour the shepherdess is otherwise perfect both in body and mind." But the Queen of Golconda was furious at the favour shown to this newcomer to the harem. She awaited her chance and when the king was away from his capital she ordered the shepherdess to be tied to a tree, her clothes drenched with oil and then set alight. She watched the sufferings of the poor girl, intending to gloat over her rival's agony; but she must have been deficient in imagination for what she saw not only surpassed her anticipations but presently filled her with remorse. The girl's "movements were so horrifying that Cruelty itself could not have beheld them without some sentiment of compassion or at any rate of horror." The Queen went out of her mind and "during the whole of the rest of her life she never ceased to tremble and go through all the motions of the shepherdess."

Shivaji's request for passage for his forces at first appalled Abu Hussein. It was not so much the presence in his dominions of so large an army (though considering the notoriety the Maratha cavalry had won throughout India, this in itself was sufficiently daunting); there was also the fear of embroilment with the Moguls on the grounds of alliance with the Maratha power, the inevitable enemy of the Empire. This second consideration weighed also with Shivaji; it was not so important to win from Golconda the friendly gesture of passage for his troops (for in fact he could easily have won such passage by sheer force); as to keep a friendly Golconda in his rear after his arrival on the south-east coast; a hostile kingdom between him and his own country, or even a weak kingdom invoking a Mogul alliance in a panic, would be fatal to the permanence of his conquests.

He was well served by his envoy to the court of Golconda, Hanmante, a Brahman with a deep interest in metaphysics and a perfect knowledge of court Persian. Before broaching his master's projects Hanmante made himself agreeable to the Golconda prime minister, like himself a Brahman, Madanna, and the two scholarly gentlemen sat together for long hours exchanging quotations from the Sanskrit classics and exploring the interminable mazes of Hindu philosophy. It was not long before Madanna was singing the praises of the Maratha king's envoy to his own King, Abu Hussein. When Hanmante was introduced to the latter, he paid his respects in beautiful Persian which so delighted the king that he invited him again and again to his palace.

Hanmante was less concerned to extract definite and binding terms from the King of Golconda than to hypnotise him with the picture of a friendly, a fascinating and an invincible Shivaji, to oppose whom in any detail would be fantastic. He succeeded so well in this that Abu Hussein became impatient to meet Shivaji in person and sent a message saying he proposed to welcome the Maratha at the frontiers of his kingdom so as to escort him with the honour due to so great a prince. Shivaji replied with equal courtesy and a certain grave irony, "I have always regarded you as an elder brother. You must not demean yourself to an inferior like me." But the prime minister advanced to welcome Shivaji and the great Maratha army marched towards Hyderabad,[1] where the Golconda court was then in residence.

The discipline of the Marathas excited astonished admiration. Shivaji had issued strict orders against foraging in Golconda territory; all provisions had to be bought and bought from willing vendors; and a formidable list of punishments was promulgated for any damage done to the villages through which the Marathas passed. On only a few occasions were any punishments found necessary. An army of seventy thousand soldiers, mostly rough hill tribesmen, marched through an undefended country of almost legendary wealth, ruled over by princes of a hated religion, with the discipline and self-denial of Cromwell's New Model. While Shivaji did lead and direct expeditions whose only object was plunder, it is only necessary to consider the advance of his

[1] The present State of His Exalted Highness, the Nizam, is the successor of the Kingdom of Golconda. The territories of Golconda were absorbed in the Mogul Empire, but split off again in the 18th century, just as the Bahmani Kingdom in the anarchy after Tughlah dynasty.

army across Golconda to reject the usual English estimate of him as a wild freebooter.

At Hyderabad Shivaji was received with wild enthusiasm. The streets of the city had been thickly sprinkled with scarlet and saffron powder and scarlet awnings hung overhead from house to house, so that one seemed to pass down endless tunnels of yellow and scarlet. From all the windows people leaned out, clasping in their hands flowers constructed of gold leaf to shower on the Maratha king, and the Hindu women held ready lighted lamps to wave over his head in sign of blessing. Shivaji responded to the welcome with a tactful abandonment of his usual robust simplicity of manner and dress. Before entering the city he donned his royal robes of silk and gold, he distributed among his officers bracelets and gold cuirasses and swords and jewelled sprays for their turbans. As he entered the main gate and the assembled crowds roared a welcome, Shivaji cast to right and left of him handfuls of gold coins and jewels and ordered his treasurer to present robes of honour to many of the citizens who pressed round his horse.

But it is unlikely that Shivaji's efforts to rival Muhammadan magnificence impressed the Golconda nobles. The pomp of their ordinary life was as great as that of the nobles of Bijapur or Agra. No gentleman of Golconda stirred out of his house without an elephant or two to precede him; banners waving above the howdahs, and fifty or sixty horsemen and trumpeters and fluteplayers, and lacqueys "carrying lances and with fine Napkins driving away the Flies."[1] The noble himself would be carried in a silver and purple palanquin, "holding Flowers in his hand, smoaking Tobacco, and showing a most supine dissoluteness"; the palanquin being surrounded by musicians riding on camels.

At the Palace Abu Hussein awaited his fascinating, dangerous guest. The Palace was a very large building "more than three hundred and four-score paces in length." In front of the main entrance was a raised portico "where the Royal Musicians came several times a day to play upon their Instruments when the King was in Town."[2] All the galleries of the Palace were adorned by fountains and every room was equipped with running water. Nevertheless the general effect was spoilt for M. Thevenot who visited Golconda shortly before Shivaji by the fact that the Palace was surrounded with "ugly shops made of Wood." However, the gardens compensated for this disappointment. They were as lovely as all Muslim gardens are—for Muhammadans have always retained their desert-dwelling ancestors' joy in the miracle of water, in flowers and trees and shade. In the gardens were "long walks kept very clean and lovely Fruit-trees. . . . It is planted with Palms and Areca-trees so near to one

[1] Thevenot. [2] *Idem.*

another that the Sun can hardly pierce through them, with borders of White Flowers which they call Flowers of David, like Camomile-Flowers; also Indian Gilly-flowers."

On Shivaji's arrival at the palace the two rulers embraced and sat down side by side on the King of Golconda's throne. Servants stood round them with trays of spices and long-necked gold spittoons. Attendants, robed in the traditional Golconda habit of stiff muslin spangled with plaques of gold, fanned them with bunches of peacock feathers. Birds sang in jewelled cages and horses, dyed blue or scarlet, their tails dusted with gold powder, were led past in procession.[1]

For several hours the two kings talked, Shivaji consciously exercising his charm to win over completely the timid Persian. The latter, who had always heard of Shivaji as a wild hill-savage, delighting only in destruction and the ruin of Islam, succumbed at once to Shivaji's courtesies and compliments. His large melancholy eyes wandered over Shivaji's face, seeking for some trace in those delicate features and in that winning smile of the demon of Muslim legend. When Shivaji rose to leave for the palace set aside for his residence in Hyderabad, Abu Hussein embraced him again, anointed his wrists with attar of roses applied with

[1] These details from Kutb-Shahi miniatures in the collection of Mr. Seddon, Reader in Persian to the University of Oxford.

a silver spoon and offered for his refreshment an envelope of pan-leaf enclosing confections of betel nut and cardamum that he had himself prepared.

For several days there were banquets and festivities, Abu Hussein every day showering on Shivaji and his captains presents of jewels, dresses, horses and war elephants. He took a childish pleasure in parading the wealth of Golconda before the eyes of the rough hillmen from the west. If he could not cap Shivaji's exploits with stories of his own daring, he could at least surprise the Maratha with refinements of luxury. He took Shivaji round his capital, pointing out the mosques and palaces and the tombs of his ancestors, great square buildings of black stone with green domes. In each of these mausoleums the sarcophagus was "covered with a Carpet and on the Tomb a Satten Pall with White Flowers trailing upon the Ground, the whole being lighted with many Lamps."[1]

One day when Shivaji expressed astonishment at the size and gorgeous trappings of the chief war-elephant of Golconda, Abu Hussein said, "But have you *no* war elephants of your own?"

Shivaji turned and pointed to some of his guardsmen who stood at attention behind him and said, "These are my war elephants."

Abu Hussein smiled, almost scornfully, and began to tell stories of how his elephant was regarded by

[1] Thevenot.

every one with terror. Shivaji nodded to one of his captains, Yesaji. "You'll find him more than a match for your elephant," he said.

"Let us see," said Abu Hussein. The war elephant's mahout slid off its back and the stable-hands incited it to fury. Yesaji advanced, his sword drawn. The elephant trumpeted and rushed towards him. Yesaji stepped aside and with a single blow severed the brute's trunk. The elephant, who for all his armour plating and military titles had experienced nothing more dangerous than mock combats in the palace gardens, fled roaring and screaming with pain. Yesaji calmly returned to his place behind Shivaji. Abu Hussein in an access of humility not only sent for new presents for Shivaji and his staff but even presented Shivaji's horse with a necklace of jewels.

Shivaji, however, required more convincing evidence of amity than presents and parties. In return for Maratha aid in case of a Mogul or Bijapur move against Golconda and for some territorial adjustments of the Golconda frontier along the Carnatic, Shivaji demanded the loan of the Golconda artillery and a greatly enhanced subsidy (as the Golconda court described the new payment of three thousand *hun* a day; tribute, the Marathas were blunt enough to call it). After long negotiations these terms were agreed on and Shivaji left Hyderabad in March and advanced rapidly towards the

Carnatic. Crossing the Krishna river, he ordered his captains to continue their march southwards. Then he slipped away from the army and, accompanied only by Hanmante, the successful Brahman envoy to Golconda, he visited a famous shrine of the god Shiva at Shri Shaila. Perhaps the festivities at Hyderabad had wearied him with their unreal glitter, for once again the old longing for a monastic life swept over him. Kneeling in the silence and gloom of the great shrine he burst into tears and lamented that he should have to pass his life in palaces and camps when he was only happy when alone and at prayer. For ten days he remained in the temple, fasting and in constant prayer. Hanmante grew anxious. He began to plead with his master, urging him to rejoin the army; the Carnatic lay open to his sword; time was precious. Shivaji cried bitterly, "But I am only happy here," and drawing his sword he added, "If I cannot live on here, at least let me die here," and he tried to fall on his sword. Hanmante caught him by the arm, begging him to remember the kingdom he was deserting, the soldiers he was leaving leaderless, the task begun and unfinished. Shivaji sighed heavily, stood motionless a moment and then sheathed his sword. He left the temple the same day, but before leaving bestowed on the priests great treasures for the cult of the god in memory of his ten days' happiness in the shrine.

He rejoined his army at Anantpur and the Maratha forces swept resistlessly over the Carnatic. The central government at Bijapur had not ventured to oppose Shivaji's march and now offered no open opposition to his seizure of the forts and towns of the east coast. A few garrisons and commanders, more resolute than the government they served, resisted the Marathas, but seldom for long. The huge fortress of Jinji, to be later revealed in Maratha hands as impregnable against Mogul assault, was taken at a rush. The Jesuit fathers at Madura paused in their congenial task of reconciling Vedantic pantheism with Christian philosophy and wrote excitedly, "Shivaji fell upon the place like a thunderbolt and carried it at the first assault." Not content with which he "constructed new ramparts, raised towers and bastions and carried out all these works with a perfection of which European skill would not have been ashamed."

Leaving a force to invest Vellore, which was defended not only by a resolute garrison of Afghans but also by a number of savage crocodiles which swarmed in the moat surrounding the city, Shivaji pressed on south. In June he came up with the Bijapur Governor of the district, who was prudently retreating before the Marathas, and in a headlong charge through a thick wood drove him in flight with only a hundred men, leaving behind the rest of his army as prisoners, together with his horses, cavalry and artillery. When within ten miles of Tanjore, Shivaji's half brother, obviously appalled at this terrifying swift approach, timidly opened negotiations. Shivaji invited him to his camp, but, distrusting his good faith, demanded that five members of his entourage should be given to Shivaji as hostages. Shortly before he had written to the English merchants in Madras desiring to purchase some "cordial stores and other sorts of Counter-Poisons."

Vyankoji was petulant and defiant. After a week of tearful wrangling he escaped by night from his brother's camp and addressed wild appeals for help to most of the princes of India, including the Great Mogul. Shivaji would have been justified had he exacted satisfaction from this gesture of renewed hostilities from Vyankoji's hostages, but he only shrugged his shoulders and said, "Why did he run off like that? He is young and has acted like a child." Then, turning towards the trembling hostages he dismissed them with presents and robes of honour.

Throughout the following year Vyankoji flitted up and down the Carnatic coast; but he had no forces to oppose to those of Shivaji and the absorption of the territories he had inherited from his father was but an incident in the general Maratha conquest of the south. When Vyankoji finally submitted Shivaji gave him the town of Tanjore and certain adjacent lands to keep him employed but imposed upon him as his minister that shrewd Brahman, Hanmante. In actual fact this nominee of Shivaji's became the real ruler of Tanjore; for Vyankoji, depressed by his defeat, abandoned the habits of his rank and adopted the life of a religious mendicant.

By 1678 not only the Carnatic but also Mysore beyond had been conquered, and leaving a large army of occupation to garrison his new dominions Shivaji returned to his capital in Western India with an enormous train of plunder. As Mr. Gary wrote from Bombay in January of that year, "With a Successe as happy as *Cæsars* in Spaine, he came, saw and reported soe vast a Treasure in Gold, Diamonds, Emeralds, Rubies and wrought Corall that have strengthened his armes with very able sinewes to prosecute his further Victorious designes."

It is easy, so apparently effortless was Shivaji's triumph, to underestimate the difficulties which the expedition presented and the skill with which Shivaji overcame them. The actual campaign had to be conducted in an unfamiliar terrain over seven hundred miles from his base. Immediate and spectacular success was essential; for a few temporary reverses would have tempted the Mogul generals to launch an offensive along the northern frontiers of the Maratha country, would have stirred Bijapur to a last despairing effort, would have clouded the bright confidence of the King of Golconda in the invincibility of his new friend. A

Mogul army overrunning Maharashtra, Bijapur and Golconda stiffened with Mogul auxiliaries and subsidies, their territories lying across the Maratha lines of communication and of retreat—such forebodings must have been a spur to Shivaji in every engagement. Yet he showed never by any impatience the strain to which the long campaign exposed him; even when a fort held out against him unexpectedly for twenty-six days, the garrison being led by the widow of the commandant who had fallen in the first Maratha assault, his reception of the martial lady on her eventual surrender was marked by his usual courtesy and she was at once set at liberty.

At the end of eighteen months the conquest of the Carnatic and of Mysore was complete and on his return to his capital Shivaji announced the annexation of a strip of Bijapur territory connecting his new conquests with the Maratha country.

It is not so much from the acquisition of territory that this campaign is important as for the subsequent strategic use of the new provinces. The Carnatic was to be the final line of Maratha defence in the event of some new vast effort of the Empire. As the Athenians abandoned their homeland for an island and their ships, so the Maratha government would, in time of need, fall back to the remote forts along the eastern coast. After the effort of subduing the Maratha country, to undertake another campaign with communications extended seven hundred miles farther on, and the *nexus* of these communications lying in the hostile if temporarily subdued Maratha country, would fatally strain even the resources of the Empire.

So Shivaji calculated and the event approved his extraordinary strategic prevision. In the last campaign of his life when Aurangzeb, after Shivaji's death, staked all the wealth and man power of the Empire in a final effort to reduce the Marathas, the Mogul armies overthrew every obstacle in their path, Golconda and Bijapur collapsing like dykes swept away in a flood, the Maratha forts falling one by one after desperate resistance, till finally Jinji was reached where Shivaji's second son Rajaram still kept alive the flame of Maratha resistance. The Jesuit fathers had admired Shivaji's fortifications of Jinji and the epic siege of that place justified their admiration. The Moguls' assaults failed; the huge Imperial armies wasted away with hunger and disease; the Emperor, weighed down with age and disillusion, staggered back towards the north, all about him the roar of rebellion and the crumbling of an empire. He turned his face to the wall and sighed out his life in bitter grief—and under his pillow was found a document concluding with the remark, "Never trust your sons and ever keep in mind the saying, '*The word of a King is barren.*'"

His body was hurried through empty streets and none of his subjects mourned his passing. He was buried in a simple grave in the little town of Ranza. And yet there was one man who remembered a certain act of kindness that Aurangzeb had done him long ago. Shivaji's grandson, now King of the Marathas, came in state to pray by Aurangzeb's grave. He wished to show his gratitude for that generous impulse that had caused Aurangzeb to grant Zinat-un-Nisa's prayer not to interfere with the young Maratha's religion.

From a beleaguered garrison the Maratha forces became the only military power of consequence in India. After Aurangzeb's death, Mogul Emperor was but a name. Maratha horsemen rode into the streets of Delhi. Maratha sentries paced down the corridors of the Imperial palaces. It was left to the English to rescue from his Maratha Odoacer a more pathetic figure than Romulus Augustulus, a lonely blind old man sitting nervously under a tattered canopy, unrecognisable as a descendant of Tamerlane.

CHAPTER TWENTY-ONE

ANY satisfaction that Shivaji felt over the success of his Carnatic expedition was soon clouded by domestic difficulties.

His return to Raigad was the signal for renewed intrigues by Queen Soyra, urging the claims to the succession of her son Rajaram. As if to justify her insinuations of Sambhaji's instability and selfish indulgence, the senior prince became involved in a discreditable intrigue with a Brahman woman. Shivaji had him arrested and confined in Panhala Fort. Reared in palaces Sambhaji had little sympathy either with his father's strenuous energy or with the simplicity of his father's subjects. When he had visited the Mogul camp at Aurangabad he found that Mogul captains dressed more splendidly and lived more comfortably than his father who called himself a king; their harems and troops of slaves contrasted agreeably with the bleak discipline of Maratha life. He took to dressing like a courtier of Delhi, white muslin skirt starched into stiff folds of such transparent material as not to hide the rich brocade tights on his shapely calves, shawls of silk embroidered with designs of flowers, a turban of heavy with jewels. In imitation of the favourite Imperial gesture he liked to hold a flower to his

fleshy nose while his large fine eyes, lacking the fire of Shivaji's and reminding one of his mother Saibai's dreamy passivity, stared vacantly about him.[1] But his moods of sensual acquiescence alternated with bursts of scarcely sane passion.

It was unlikely that he would patiently bear his arrest and imprisonment. He sent a letter to the Mogul Commander-in-Chief, Dilir Khan (Jai Sing's choleric subordinate in the 1665 campaign, he who, learning of the easy terms granted to Shivaji, had torn at his wrist with his teeth), and receiving a cordial reply, Sambhaji escaped from Panhala Fort and took refuge in Mogul territory. He was warmly received by Dilir Khan who gave him a dress of honour and offered him the command of seven thousand horse. Dilir Khan wrote to Delhi suggesting that Sambhaji should be recognised by the Emperor as King of the Marathas; for he hoped that this would divide the Marathas into two factions.

It was improbable that this hope would be realised since Shivaji was worshipped by the nation he had created and Sambhaji had very few adherents; nevertheless, Dilir Khan's suggestion was natural; one recognises the procedure and reasoning usually applied by Imperialist governments in relation to frontier states. But Aurangzeb, as usual, began to suspect his subject's good faith. Why was Dilir Khan so anxious to advance Sambhaji's cause?—

[1] Details from miniatures in the Parasnis collection.

Sambhaji, too, who had been at Agra with his father and like him had escaped. So Aurangzeb ordered Dilir Khan to arrest Sambhaji and bring him as a prisoner to Delhi. Dilir Khan—either because he foresaw a long period of doubt and indecision ending in the death of the Maratha prince whom he had welcomed and to whom he had given hospitality, or because he was afraid that Sambhaji might escape a second time from Aurangzeb's clutches and then he, Dilir Khan, would fall under Imperial displeasure—began making such ostentatious preparations for Sambhaji's arrest and addressing Sambhaji in a new insulting manner as though a jailer to his prisoner, that Sambhaji took the hint and fled back to his father. So Dilir Khan could claim that Sambhaji had broken his parole and escaped just in time to avoid arrest. Shivaji received his son without reproaches, embraced him and addressed him with affection. But he would not restore him to official favour and admit him to the court.

The breach between them was never healed, for when Shivaji was on his deathbed, Sambhaji seems not to have been immediately informed of his father's sudden illness. When he heard, he mounted his swiftest camel and rode without resting from Panhala to Raigad, through the long day and stifling night of an Indian hot weather, only to learn when he reached the fort of Raigad hill that his father was dead. He turned on his camel and cut off

its head. Then he ordered that a statue of a headless camel should be raised on that spot to mark his dramatic exhibition of disappointment and grief. This monument of a not very sensible action is still standing.

If Sambhaji's character formed a sad contrast to that of his father, Marathas have forgiven him for his unfilial faithlessness because of his terrible death and his constancy to his faith. He was ordered by the Emperor to embrace Islam. He refused and was made to run the gauntlet of the whole Imperial army. Tattered and bleeding he was brought before the Emperor and repeated his refusal. His tongue was torn out and again the question was put. He called for writing materials and wrote, "Not even if the Emperor bribed me with his daughter." So then he was put to death by torture. Imperial revenge helped Sambhaji to expiate his many faults.

The last year of Shivaji's life was marked by his appearance in a new rôle, that of defender of Bijapur. That unhappy city was disturbed by constant faction-fights. The Sultan was a minor and the Queen-Mother, unlike the determined lady who had sent Afzul Khan against Shivaji, was accused even by her son of frivolous and unbecoming conduct; she cruised about the Arabian sea with more than Caroline-like publicity, misconducting

herself with Dutch sailors, for whom in her old age she had discovered a sudden taste.[1] A quarrel over an alleged promise to give a Bijapur princess to one of Aurangzeb's sons developed into a dreary war between Bijapur and the Empire. Dilir Khan advanced on Bijapur and invested the city, completing the ruin and disintegration of all Bijapur territory outside the walls of the city. Insistence on imperial dignity and prestige was completing the Balkanisation of Muhammadan India and rendering inevitable Maratha domination.

An interesting feature of this siege was the number of experiments in plastic surgery made by the Mogul surgeons. The citizens of Bijapur cut off the noses of all Moguls they caught and certain army doctors with the Imperial forces restored the missing noses with skin from the wounded men's foreheads. Manucci notes, "I saw many persons with such noses and they were not so disfigured as they would have been without any nose at all, but they bore between their eyebrows the marks of incision."

The struggle was conducted with great bitterness, the Bijapuris increasingly desperate. At last the Regent of Bijapur appealed to Shivaji. There is pathos in the phrasing of the Regent's cry for aid to the "Inhuman Butcherly fellow" of a few years ago. "You know the condition of this

[1] Bernier.

kingdom," the Regent wrote, "we have no army, no money, no ally to help us. Our enemies are numerous and avid for war. . . . We cannot defend ourselves, unless you help us. Turn towards us. Tell us what we should do and we will do it."

Shivaji first required recognition of all his conquests in Southern India and of all the districts he had detached by force from Bijapur. When this was agreed to, Shivaji sent two of his captains who first cut to pieces a Mogul force marching to reinforce Dilir Khan, and then broke up Dilir Khan's siege-train and drove his army away from the walls of Bijapur back to Mogul territory. Dilir Khan had, as a subordinate, seen Shivaji's humiliation by Jai Sing. Now, as generalissimo, he was easily defeated by a subordinate of Shivaji. The change in the Maratha attitude to the once-dreaded Moguls could hardly be better exemplified than by the remark of Shivaji's captain, who, when given command against Dilir Khan, said gaily, "I shall go and punish Dilir Khan as he deserves."

Bijapur was now, in effect, as much a vassal state as Golconda. But the people of Bijapur (as opposed to the government) only thought of Shivaji as their deliverer in the recent siege, and when Shivaji visited Bijapur to ride in triumph through the streets, where as a boy he had wandered, a distrustful, lonely rustic, he was welcomed with wild enthusiasm and adored as almost divine.

In the Shrine of the Relic, bowing before the Casket of the Two Hairs of the Prophet, under the unchanging smiles of Venuses and Cupids, the priests who had formerly exhausted their armoury of malediction now offered prayers for Shivaji's safety and prosperity. The rich merchants in their "Turbats of Gold Damask'ed" and their "Gold Atlas Coats to their heels," who had once cursed Shivaji as a bandit interfering with the caravan routes, now bent over their carved blackwood balconies and cheered Shivaji as the hero who had saved them from Mogul sack. And as Shivaji rode into the Palace courtyard, and the courtiers in the balconies of the Water Pavilion rose at his approach and the Sultan came out most respectfully to welcome his guest to a great banquet in his honour, Shivaji must have thought of the day forty-two years before when his father introduced him into that Palace and a Sultan waited impatiently for an uncouth village lad to prostrate himself before the throne. The Maratha who had then refused obeisance now sat in pomp, waited on timidly by a Sultan. In another throne-room in the north where the same Maratha had been similarly defiant, another Maratha[1] would one day exercise authority while an Emperor meekly attended him.

Banquet followed banquet. There were reviews and processions and fêtes.

[1] Shindia, ancestor of the present Maharajah of Gwalior.

But people noticed that even at the height of victory celebrations Shivaji's face remained sad those and thoughtful. He made his excuses and slipped away from Bijapur as soon as he could. While most men would have been pardonably exalted at this strange reversal of fate—the neglected child, the rebel, the lifelong enemy welcomed now at last with servile adulation—all this made Shivaji more than ever conscious of the impermanence of everything, the change, the ending.

One last adventure showed, however, that Shivaji's old daring was not yet extinguished. Prince Muazzam, in despair at his father's continual rebukes, abandoned his former objections to treachery and evolved an elaborate plot to capture Shivaji. If Shivaji, he argued, would help Bijapur against the Empire, he would help a Mogul prince rebelling against the Emperor. So he proposed to stage a mock rebellion and ask Shivaji to come and help him; once in the Mogul camp Shivaji would be an easy victim. It was not a very hopeful scheme and Shivaji's spies were soon aware of it. One day when the Prince was returning to his camp from a hunting expedition, an old peasant standing by the roadside saluted very humbly and offered the Prince a jar of fresh milk. Muazzam was thirsty and accepted the milk gratefully. When he had drunk it he found a note at the bottom of the jar. "I, Shivaji, present this jar of milk and if there is anything else I can do for you, I am at your service." Muazzam looked up and, of course, the supposititious peasant had disappeared. It was Shivaji's way of letting Prince Muazzam know that he had learnt all the details of the plot.[1]

When Shivaji returned to his capital, his friends noticed a new gravity of his tone, a gentleness and resignation. To one he would turn suddenly and ask to be forgiven for any mistakes he might have been guilty of, for any failing or fault; to another he would speak gravely of his country's future after his death, of his foolish son, Sambhaji, and the strong, bitter Soyra. Wearied by the intrigues of the Queen-Consort, for the benefit of whose son he had many times refused to alter the succession in spite of Sambhaji's defects, Shivaji no longer visited the apartments of his women-folk. Queen Soyra complained bitterly, "I have dealt faithfully with him from my childhood. But now he had no affection for me. That is why he has left me and sleeps alone."[2] She offered a prize to any one who could provide her with a love philtre to win back his affections. But nothing could wean Shivaji from his increasing melancholy. He wrote to Ramdas: "It were good if God would summon me to His feet. I cannot longer bear being separated from my mother."[3]

[1] Manucci. [2] Shivadigvijaya. Translated by S. N. Sen. [3] *Idem.*

The foreboding of his approaching death increased, and when in March, 1680, a painful swelling on his knee made walking troublesome, he took to his couch with resignation. His knee grew swollen and inflamed and soon he fell into a high fever.

By April 3rd it was clear he was dying. His captains and ministers stood round his couch lamenting. He roused himself from his stupor to beg them not to weep, reminding them that death came equally to all and that their religion promised immortality.

While the Queen's apartments were full of uneasy whispers, of threats and hints and expressions of foreboding, there was calm and stillness in Shivaji's room as the Brahmans filed in to give him final absolution. In the words of the prescribed ritual they asked him, "Why have you summoned us?" And the dying man replied, "I have not ceased from sin from my birth until this moment. Do you absolve me and free me from the burden of my sins." One Brahman, he who is known as the Scapegoat, then, after prayer, said, "Except such grievous sins as murder and adultery, I take on myself your sins and free you from them." They prayed again and anointed him with holy water from the Ganges, and asked him to make the final confession of Hindu faith. When he had done so they scattered over his couch leaves of sacred basil.[1]

[1] For the deathbed and funerary rites of a Maratha, see *Tribes and Castes of the Bombay Presidency*. (Bom. Govt. Press and Bom. Gazetteer.)

Presently he died.

They took his sword and placed it in the temple of the Mother-Goddess at Satara where it may be seen to-day. The attendants bring it out from the shadows of the inner shrine. Drawn from its sheath, the sword seems enormous and most unwieldy. The archaic simplicity of its design is a strange contrast to the tawdry decorations of the temple where it is housed, the artificial flowers and cut-glass chandeliers. It "has been to the Maratha bards what the Joyeuse and Durand of Charlemagne and Roland and the Askalon of our own patron saint were to the wandering troubadours of Europe."[1]

When the news reached Delhi, Aurangzeb, though his face lit up with joy, was yet stirred to a speech of unusual chivalry. "He was a great captain and the only one who has had the magnanimity to raise a new Kingdom. My armies have been employed against him for nineteen years, and, nevertheless, his state has been always increasing." (Orme).

The more general Mogul feeling was better expressed by the historian, Khafi Khan, who exclaimed, "The infidel has gone to hell."[2]

The English, however, took long to be convinced that the extraordinary Maratha could really be dead. Bombay wrote to Surat, "We have certaine news that Sevagee Rajah is dead," but Surat, replying on

[1] Sullivan, quoted in Parasnis' *Mahabaleshwar*.

[2] This expression has, besides its concise appropriateness, the further advantage of being an anagram on the date of Shivaji's death.

the 7th of May, was more cautious, "Sevagee's death is confirmed from all places; yet some are under a doubt of the truth, such reports having been used to run of him before some considerable attempt. Therefore you shall not be too confident until better assured."

Eight months after his death they were still writing in Bombay, "Sevagee had dyed so often that some begine to thincke him immortelle. 'Tis certaine little beliefe can be given of his death till experience shews it per the waning of his hitherto prosperous affaires, since when he dies *indeed*, it is thought he has none to leave behind him that is capacitated to carry on things at that rate and fortune he has all along done."

But dead the king was, dead in his Palace at Raigad, that restless spirit stilled at last.

The murmur of the huge crowds collected to do homage to the Liberator on his last journey—the chanting of priests and the quiet prayers of the Palace mourners who, as they swung their censers, scattering handfuls of mustard seed to avert the assaults of demons, ejaculated at intervals in accordance with Hindu funerary rites, "Victory! Victory!"—the hammering at the funeral pyre that was being raised beyond the Palace gates on a mound from which the flames would be visible for many leagues—all these noises hardly penetrated the little room where Shivaji lay, fragrant bilva leaves for his mattress and rose petals for coverlet. The eyes whose brilliance all had remarked on were closed. The mouth that had so often opened in laughter was thin and sunken now. Under the tongue that had so often charmed, encouraged and inspired, they had placed a single emerald.

Reverently they covered his face with a white cloth, having a round hole over the mouth, and through this hole they let fall a few drops of holy water. In token of mourning they had shaved their heads and pared their nails to the quick. They placed at the dead man's feet the long hair that his women-folk had cut off and they scattered rose petals over him. Then they placed him in a great palanquin of state and bore him out of the Palace, away from the shuttered and darkened rooms and the wailing of the women, out into the yellow light of late afternoon. The spear grass was brown from the hot April suns, the trees stark and scorched. From the Palace walls one saw a vast wilderness of bare outcrops of rock, blue precipices and shadowed ravines and in the far distance the glitter of the sea. As they bore him between the ranks of mourners the sobs, stifled in obedience to Hindu ritual, were like the sound of a forest straining under a strong wind.

They laid the body on the pyre, the head towards the north, towards the Himalayas where Shiva reigns in glory with his bride, the Daughter of the Snow.

They walked round the pyre scattering rice grains and coconut shavings. Then they set alight to the pyre. Only when the body was consumed might the mourners give rein to their grief and lament aloud, striking the palms of their hands upon their open mouths. It was already evening and the stars were coming out.

THE END

AUTHORITIES

Orme: *Historical Fragments of the Mogul Empire and of the Morattoes.*

Bernier: *Travels in the Mogul Empire.* (Tr. Constable.)

Manucci: *Storia do Mogul.* (Tr. Irvine.)

Irvine: *Army of the Indian Moguls.*

Fryer: *New Account of India.*

De Læt: *Topography of the Mogul Empire.*

Rawlinson: *Shivaji the Maratha; English Beginnings in Western India.*

Sarkar: *Historical Essays; History of Aurangzeb; Anecdotes of Aurangzeb; The India of Aurangzeb.*

Kincaid & Parasnis: *History of the Maratha People.*

Khafi Khan's *History.* (Tr. Elliot and Dowson.)

Gazetteer of Bombay Presidency and Gazetteer of India: *Tribes and Castes of the Bombay Presidency.* (Bombay Government Press.)

Ranade: *Rise of the Maratha Power.*

Grant Duff: *History of the Marathas.*

Oxford History of India. (Vincent Smith.)

Thompson and Garratt: *Rise and Fulfilment of British Rule in India.*

Pietro della Valle: *Travels.*

Cousens: *Bijapur.*

Foster: *English Factories in India.*

Archæological Survey of India. Vols. XXXVII and XXXI.

D. B. Parasnis: *Mahabaleshwar; Panhala; Poona.*

Hedge's Diary. (Ed. Yule.)

European Travellers to India. E. F. Oates. (Maclehose.)

Purchas: *Hakluytus.* Posthumous.

Broughton: *Letters written in a Maratha Camp.*

Tavernier: *Travels.*
Thevenot: *Travels.*
Keene: *Agra.*
Latif: *Agra.*
Howell: *Agra.*
Scott Waring: *History of the Mahrathas.*
Morland: *From Akbar to Aurangzeb.*
Karkaria: *Death of Shivaji; Episode of Shivaji and Afzul Khan.*
Lane-Poole: *Medieval India; Aurangzeb.*
Acworth: *Ballads of the Marathas.*
Dellon: *Travels in East Indies and Madagascar.*
Surendranath Sen: *Administrative System of the Marathas; Shivaji Chatrapati; Military System of the Marathas.*
Letters of Aurangzeb. (Ed. and Transl. by T. Bilimoria.)
Gemelli Careri: *Voyage autour du Monde.*
Anon: *Present State of Native Powers in India.*
Enthoven: *Folklore of the Bombay Presidency.*